2024 Wood Dragon Year
FENG SHUI
AND CHINESE ASTROLOGY PLANNER

MICHELE CASTLE

Welcome to the energies of the Wood Dragon in 2024! This year is under the influence of the majestic Wood Dragon, a symbol of bold fortune. Dragons are captivating creatures known for their confidence and charm, though they can occasionally be vain and proud. Nevertheless, their allure is undeniable, and they possess an unquenchable thirst for novelty, often displaying boundless energy, vivacity, and a penchant for social gatherings.

The Wood Dragon of 2024 epitomises these traits, acting as a trendsetter and leader, exuding sophistication and style. These quintessential Dragon characteristics will be prominently intertwined with the year's energy.

In 2024, the Dragon aligns with the Wood element, signifying a time ripe for fresh beginnings, hard work, and the potential for substantial growth and prosperity. Wood, revered as the progenitor of the Fire element, holds the power to ignite passion, stimulate creativity, inspire innovation, and introduce novel concepts.

The 2024 Astrology & Feng Shui diary provides daily insights into your health, relationships, and business opportunities, offering valuable guidance from Chinese Astrology, Flying Star, and the Bagua School.

Embrace the changes and energies that 2024 has in store:

A year of action and transformation.

A time for optimism and empathy.

A period characterised by movement and determination.

Anticipate unforeseen shifts and surprising developments.

While Feng Shui doesn't possess magical remedies, understanding and strategic placement of symbolic cures can help reduce vulnerability in these uncertain times. Embracing the profound science of Feng Shui empowers you to adapt more effectively to the evolving energies in your environment, home, and the world. Feng Shui translates to "wind and water," symbolising the essence of life's energy and fluidity.

May 2024 usher in health, harmony, and prosperity as you navigate existence's dynamic winds and flowing waters.

Published by Complete Feng Shui
Mb: 0421 116 799,
Email: info@completefengshui.com.au
Websites: www.completefengshui.com

2024 Feng Shui & Astrology Planner 2024 ©

Text copyright © Michele Castle

Illustrations copyright © Michele Castle / Lucy Deslandes

All rights reserved. No part of this publication may be reproduced, stored in a retrieval system or transmitted in any form or by any means, electronic, mechanical, photocopying, recording, or otherwise, without the prior written permission from Complete Feng Shui.

The author's moral right to be identified as the author of this book has been asserted.

Author: Michele Castle

Design copyright @completefengshui

Title: 2024 Feng Shui & Astrology Planner

ISBN: 978-0-6459620-9-3 (Paperback)

ISBN: 978-0-6459097-1-5 (eBook)

December 2023

This Planner has been written to offer insight and planning for daily activities and energies in 2024 from Flying Stars, Bagua, Chinese astrology, and date selection. The author, editor and publisher take no responsibility for the outcome of any information implemented from this Planner.

The information in this planner is summarised from the Chinese Thousand Year Calendar, presented user-friendly to help you enjoy prosperity throughout the year.

Vice President of the Association of Feng Shui Consultants (AFSC)
Platinum member of the Association of Feng Shui Consultants (AFSC)
Recognised Feng Shui training institution by the (AFSC)

facebook@completefengshui   instagram@completefengshui

CONTENTS

Personal details vii

Resolutions for 2024 ix

2024 Year of Wood Dragon 1

Chinese New Year Traditions 3

Auspicious Feng Shui Colours for 2024 5

How to Use the Complete Feng Shui Planner 7

Flying Star Feng Shui 8

Favourable Stars / Unfavourable Stars 9

2024 Afflictions 10

January 6 – February 3 is month of the Ox 12

January Flying Stars 14

January Monthly Chinese Zodiac Overview 16

The Feng Shui of Your Front Door 20

February 4 – March 5 is month of the Tiger 24

February Flying Stars 26

February Monthly Chinese Zodiac Overview 28

March 6 – April 4 is month of the Rabbit 34

March Flying Stars 36

March Monthly Chinese Zodiac Overview 38

April 5 – May 5 is month of the Dragon 44

April Flying Stars 46

April Monthly Chinese Zodiac Overview 48

Feng Shui Principles of the Bedroom 52

May 6 – June 5 is month of the Snake 56

May Flying Stars 58

May Monthly Chinese Zodiac Overview 60

June 6 – July 6 is month of the Horse 66

June Flying Stars 68

June Monthly Chinese Zodiac Overview 70

July 7 – August 7 is month of the Goat 76

July Flying Stars 78

July Monthly Chinese Zodiac Overview 80

August 8 – September 7 is month of the Monkey 86

August Flying Stars 88

August Monthly Chinese Zodiac Overview 90

Ideal Kitchen placement in Feng Shui 94

September 8 – October 7 is month of the Rooster 98

September Flying Stars 100

September Monthly Chinese Zodiac Overview 102

Activating Peach Blossom luck for relationship & marriage luck 106

October 8 – November 6 is month of the Dog 110

October Flying Stars 112

October Monthly Chinese Zodiac Overview 114

November 7 – December 6 is month of the Pig 120

Eight Aspirations Formula 121

November Flying Stars 122

November Monthly Chinese Zodiac Overview 124

December 7 – January 5 is month of the Rat 130

December Flying Stars 132

December Monthly Chinese Zodiac Overview 134

Activating Feng Shui in the Garden 138

Your Kua Number 142

Auspicious and Inauspicious directions based on your Kua Number 147

Calendar 2024 148

Calendar 2025 149

Planner 2024 150

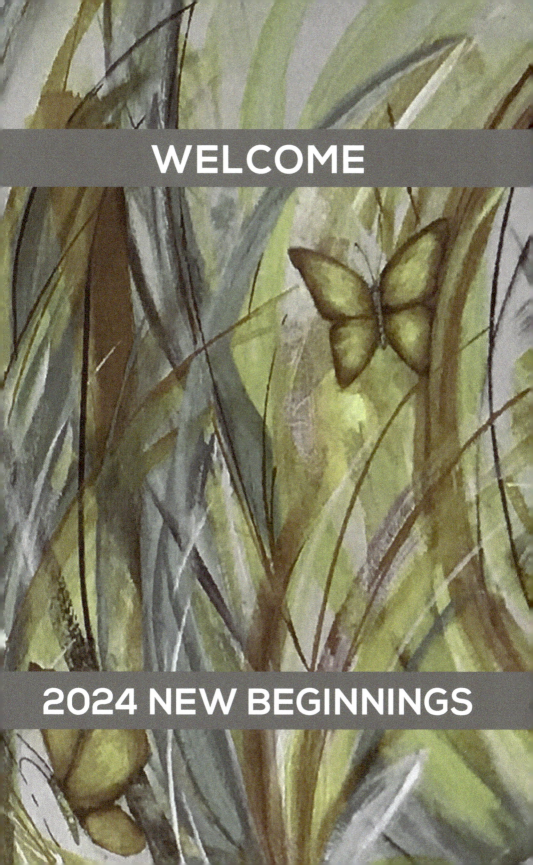

Your Personal Information

Name ....

Date of Birth ....

Time of Birth ....

Animal Sign ....

Address ....

....

....

Telephone No. .... Office No. ....

Mobile No .... Fax No. ....

E-mail address ....

Favorite Websites ....

....

Secret Friend .... Allies ....

Conflict Animal ....

Peach Blossom Animal ....

Self-Element ....

Kua Number ....

Your House Facing Direction ....

Office Direction ....

Best Direction (Sheng Chi) .... Health Direction (Tien Yi) ....

Romance Direction (Nien Yen) .... Personal Growth Direction (Fu Wei) ....

Unlucky (Ho Hai) .... Five Ghost (Wu Kwei) ....

Six Killings (Lui Sha) .... Total Loss (Chueh Ming) ....

Resolutions for 2024

....
....
....
....
....
....
....
....
....
....
....
....
....
....
....
....

In Chinese mythology, the dragon is a revered symbol of unmatched power, protection, and various auspicious qualities. It embodies strength and the force of nature, serving as a guardian against harm and evil forces. Dragons bring good luck and prosperity, often gracing celebrations with their blessings. Associated with water, they symbolise harmony and balance in nature. Historically tied to the emperor's authority, dragons signify imperial power. They are known for their transformative abilities, linking them to spiritual realms. They also represent the concept of Yin and Yang and are associated with longevity and immortality. The Chinese dragon symbolises a multifaceted blend of power, protection, and cultural significance.

2024 YEAR OF WOOD DRAGON

The Year of the Wood Dragon in 2024 brings a thirst for knowledge, a drive to embark on new ventures, a curiosity for creative and aesthetic pursuits, unshakable self-confidence, and an unending passion for celebrations and travel. But it's crucial to note immediately: the Dragon has no patience for procrastinating complainers. Beware those who dwell in the past, holding onto unrealistic hopes of miracles. In the Dragon's eyes, only action and productivity matter. You'll need to be willing to dig deep into seemingly barren ground to uncover the hidden treasures within. While earning the Wood Dragon's favour may require sustained effort, the rewards are boundless, and its generosity knows no bounds. Those seeking excitement and significant achievements would do well to embrace the qualities associated with the Wood Dragon to receive its blessings. Following the Dragon's lead, every action taken, whether with good or ill intentions, will have a spectacular and theatrical outcome, for better or worse.

In 2024, the Chinese horoscope predicts a flourishing of arts and culture, particularly in theatre, cinema, music, and graphic arts. For those in writing and visual professions, this year promises profound changes in their artistic practices. The Dragon's vibrant and revolutionary energy offers an initiatory journey to aspiring artists, guiding them to profound, challenging spiritual experiences essential for creating an aesthetic that resonates with the core of human existence.

Is 2024 a fortunate year? According to the Chinese horoscope, 2024 is unequivocally favourable for individuals born in the Year of the Dragon, the Year of the Rat, the Year of the Rooster, and the Year of the Monkey.

Apart from the Dragon, the three luckiest signs for 2024 are the compatibility triangle of the year's animal: The Rat focused on solidifying material comfort. The Rooster is actively preparing for a return to the spotlight. The Monkey, aspiring to overcome past challenges.

For other Chinese zodiac signs, especially those not aligned with the Wood element (Ox, Snake, Horse, Dog), it's advised not to overestimate their capabilities and to tackle one task at a time, both in career and relationships. While the Dragon brings luck and success to those who adhere to its principles, it also has a self-sufficient nature. Consequently, in times of trouble, help may be scarce for those in need, as the Dragon can display intolerance, selfishness, and megalomania, often cooperating only when its interests are at stake.

Yang Wood is the element of influence in 2024; for Chinese zodiac signs aligned with the Wood element, 2024 promises abundant vitality and energy for a harmonious year.

Green will be the luckiest colour in 2024; spring green, an exceptionally bright shade, is the favoured colour for the Year of the Dragon in 2024. Spring, apple, and lime green will trend in fashion and accessories throughout the Year.

Love in the Year of the Dragon 2024 forecasts joyful and enduring marriages. A union during this Year is considered auspicious in Asia. While the Dragon brings luck and generosity, it's essential to avoid being carried away by enthusiasm.

Work career, financial and social relations in 2024 is promising, especially for businesses. The Dragon's indomitable will is critical to success through diligent work, even in solitude.

World society and politics will have many advancements in AI that have blurred the lines between imitation and inspiration, raising ethical questions. Those who harness AI creatively may thrive.

Generally, 2024 fosters cultural celebrations, initiatory tourism, and political engagement. Optimism prevails as society seeks change. Environmental concerns gain prominence, with humanity addressing ecological challenges with vision and determination, aiming to reinvent the world. This is the Dragon's influence at play.

CHINESE NEW YEAR TRADITIONS

Key Practices:

Thoroughly clean your home, removing all clutter.

Keep away old brooms and brushes, replacing them with new ones to avert bad luck.

Settle existing debts if possible.

Reconcile any conflicts with family, friends, neighbours, and business partners.

Preparations, Customs, and Superstitions:

Use fresh red envelopes (ang pows) and new banknotes.

Stock up on Mandarin oranges.

Display a circular candy tray.

Decorate with flowers like plum blossom, peach blossom, and pussy willow, symbolising happiness and good fortune.

Wear new clothes and shoes for the occasion.

Lunar Chinese New Year Etiquette:

Greet others with "Gong Xi Fa Cai" to wish them a prosperous New Year.

Prepare food in advance to avoid using sharp tools on New Year's Day to preserve luck.

Maintain a positive, joyful atmosphere, refraining from negative expressions.

Avoid washing your hair on the first day of the New Year, as it's associated with washing away prosperity.

Stick to bright, auspicious colours like red and gold while avoiding white and black.

Exchange Mandarin oranges when visiting, and unmarried individuals receive Hong Baos (Ang POWS) for good luck.

Embracing Lunar Chinese New Year's Significance

Chinese New Year, Lunar Day 1, 2024, falling on February 10th, is a pivotal moment in Chinese culture. The belief is that initiating the year with precise actions, timing, and direction can invite good fortune and prosperity for the year ahead. The tradition involves selecting a specific direction to welcome auspicious stars through prayer offerings from 12:00 a.m. to 12:59 a.m. These stars are aligned with distinct purposes: Wealth resides in the Southeast, the Northeast is for Happiness, the Southwest symbolises Nobility and Patronage, and the West is the doorway to Good Luck. This practice reflects Chinese customs' rich tapestry and deep-rooted connection to auspicious beginnings.

UNVEILING THE CLASH IN 2024

Chinese astrology identifies four Zodiac signs that clash with the Annual Ruling Sign each year. In 2024, these clashing signs are the Dog, Dragon, Ox, and Goat, collectively known as "Treasure Boxes" in this realm. The severity of these clashes varies depending on an individual's Ba Zi chart. The impact can be more pronounced if two or more Clashing signs are present. The Dog sign faces the most significant challenge due to a direct clash with the Dragon sign, potentially introducing changes or obstacles. Individuals with these signs should maintain a low profile, exercise caution, and avoid impulsive decisions to mitigate potential negative consequences, including accidents, conflicts, scandals, health issues, divorce, or financial setbacks.

DECODING THE SIGNIFICANCE OF THE 2024 CLASHES

In 2024, different Chinese Zodiac signs face various types of clashes, each with its recommended resolutions:

For the Dragon, it's a conflict clash; the key is maintaining humility and avoiding conflicts of interest.

The Dog experiences a direct clash and should opt for a low-profile approach, steering clear of adventure, rulebreaking, and prioritising personal safety.

If you're a Ox, you encounter an offending clash, making it vital to stay low-key and avoid confrontations and rule-breaking while focusing on personal well-being.

Those born under the Goat sign deal with a penalty clash, which requires self-discipline, flexibility, and vigilance against betrayal issues.

DISCOVERING THE MOST COMPATIBLE SIGN IN 2024

Each year, one of the 12 zodiac signs aligns harmoniously with the ruling zodiac sign, often referred to as "The Grand Duke" or Tai Shui. In 2024, the Rooster sign claims this favourable position. Per ancient beliefs, carrying a Rooster emblem or symbol can help ward off potential metaphysical ill-effects and foster greater harmony and positive energy in your everyday life.

Secret Friends for Your Aid

Secret Friends, zodiac signs that provide support and compatibility, can help counter the metaphysical challenges stemming from clashes with the Grand Duke. They are also believed to attract helpful and supportive individuals into your life. The Secret Friend pairings for the Chinese Lunar Zodiac signs are as follows:

Rat: Ox, Dragon, Monkey

Rabbit: Dog, Pig, Goat

Horse: Goat, Tiger, Dog

Rooster: Snake, Ox, Dragon

Ox: Rat, Snake, Rooster

Dragon: Rooster, Monkey, Rat

Goat: Horse, Rabbit, Pig

Dog: Rabbit, Horse, Tiger

Tiger: Pig, Dog, Horse

Snake: Monkey, Rooster, Ox

Monkey: Rat, Dragon, Snake

Pig: Tiger, Goat, Rabbit

AUSPICIOUS FENG SHUI COLOURS FOR 2024

Discover the auspicious Feng Shui colours for 2024, the Year of the Wood Dragon in Chinese astrology. This year's primary lucky colours, spring green and imperial yellow, are influenced by the elemental themes of Wood and Earth, enhancing luck when used in clothing, accessories, or energy stones. Feng Shui principles consider the annual Flying Stars' positions and room-specific dynamics, guiding interior decor and furniture placement to align with desired energies.

In 2024, each colour will carry specific meanings associated with favoured activities and potential risks.

Blue represents peace and freedom, which is ideal for negotiations and job interviews. However, be cautious of its potential to evoke coldness and laziness, as it's associated with the Water element.

Green symbolises creativity, healing, and expansion, making it ideal for embarking on new journeys like starting a new job or moving. However, be wary of its potential to lead to madness or envy, as it's associated with the Wood element.

Red signifies vital momentum, passion, and love, making it suitable for romantic encounters and celebrating the anticipation of a new baby. But beware of its potential for danger and anger, as it's linked to the Fire element.

Yellow embodies clairvoyance, organisation, and learning, favouring real estate transactions and asset transfers. However, be cautious of its potential for deceit and vanity, as it's tied to the Earth element.

White represents precision, resistance, and equity, making it suitable for commerce, banking, and territorial defence activities. However, be alert to its potential for sorrow and defamation, as it's associated with the Metal element.

To maximise the efficacy of Lucky Colours of 2024, it's recommended to consider them in mobile contexts, such as personal accessories, vehicles, luggage, or bags, rather than static settings like homes or workplaces.

In 2024, harness the ideal annual colours for each of the 12 Chinese zodiac signs to balance the unique Dragon and Wood Yang energy blend. These colours provide protection, boost energy, and attract good fortune, mitigating potential challenges and enhancing determination and success.

Rat:	Tomato Red, Pale Green
Tiger:	Aquamarine, Azure White
Dragon:	Coral Red, Yellow Gold
Horse:	Light Green, Yellow
Monkey:	Seashell White, Khaki Yellow
Dog:	Light Orange, Peach White
Ox:	Light Gray, Olive Green
Rabbit:	Royal Blue, Grass Green
Snake:	Medium Purple, Olive Green
Goat:	Purple, Turquoise
Rooster:	Straw Yellow, Deep Sky Blue
Pig:	Lavender White, Warm Pink"

Fashion Trends in 2024, under the influence of the Wood Dragon, 2024 embraces an energy period characterised by dialogue, listening, and sharing. Yellow and green, the prominent lucky and refreshing colours for the year, extend their influence on fashion, decor, and wedding ceremonies. With the Wood Dragon's governance, the year is marked by artistic revival, eclecticism, and pride in accomplishments, even those left unfinished. The collective spirit leans towards increased cooperation among individuals. In fashion, brands are transitioning toward more sustainable models, exploring forgotten or novel materials like hemp and seaweed leather and adopting eco-friendly dyeing and printing techniques to reduce environmental impact.

The Wood element amplifies creative and pragmatic impulses driven by a desire for deliberate and determined change. With the Wood Dragon at the helm, even the wildest dreams become attainable, provided one maintains consistency and avoids distractions. Conflicts are subdued, disagreements find resolution, and a truce is declared for negotiations and renewed dialogue. As the predominant energy of 2024, the Wood element encourages all Chinese zodiac signs to reevaluate the core aspects of their life experiences through the lens of unbridled creativity. The convergence of cultures fosters a fruitful, playful, and optimistic discourse in a world undergoing profound transformation.

How to use the Complete Feng Shui Diary

Clarity and good timing are vital in ensuring that whatever you undertake is given the best possible chance of success. Even simple everyday activities can have substantial adverse outcomes if riddled with obstacles and bad energy.

ACTIVITY ICONS travelling, moving, renovating, or signing a contract

This diary contains specially calculated auspicious dates for significant activities like travelling, moving, renovating or breaking ground, or signing a contract. Icons on each page mark these.

Understanding The Icons

FAVOURABLE DAYS FOR SPECIFIC TASKS

The icons on each page reveal favourable days for travelling, love and relationship luck, moving house, signing contracts, starting construction and renovating.

Unfavourable days are also indicated for any significant activities on clash days.

CHINESE ASTROLOGY ANIMALS

Each day's summary includes good /bad days for certain animal signs. When undertaking any significant activity, always check whether it is a good/bad day for your sign, as this overrides whatever the icons indicate. E.g., if it is a bad day for the Dragon, then all activities will NOT be auspicious for the Dragon that day, no matter what the icons indicate. The Dragon must avoid scheduling important matters that day.

FLYING STAR FENG SHUI

Getting your Feng Shui right for the coming year and energising the promising sectors in 2024 will help ensure smooth sailing and a prosperous year ahead.

As we move from one year to the next, energy changes. Transforming from Yin to Yang, from element to element, from one animal sign to the next. Depending on the ruling element and animal, the energy in the home and its occupants also changes from one month to the next. Time exerts a powerful impact on your Feng Shui, luck, and destiny.

Good Feng Shui cannot and does not last forever. It must be recharged with small but significant changes every year. Energy must be refreshed, reorganised and re-energised. Spaces and places need rejuvenation. Energy must be kept moving.

The Flying Stars formula of Feng Shui is a technical approach that directly addresses the effect of time on the energy of homes and businesses and holds a beautiful promise that enables you to improve your luck tremendously. The 2024 Feng Shui chart maps out the distribution of energy in each of the eight sectors of the compass, as well as the centre.

The best strategy is to take care of the negative Stars first and then concentrate on boosting the good ones. Pay closer attention to the sectors where your main door, living room and bedrooms are located. The luck in the main entrance and living room sector affects everyone in the household, while the bedroom alters the fate of those who sleep in it.

The Flying Star energy undergoes annual changes, and a dominant star positioned at the centre of the Lo Shu chart governs the overall energy for the year. In 2024, the reigning Flying Star is the 3, while different stars influence specific sectors. For instance, the NW is impacted by the Flying Star 4, the West by the Flying Star 5, and so on. Additionally, the Flying Stars' energy varies monthly as a new star joins the annual stars, influencing each month's energy. You can find a monthly overview at the start of each month. Furthermore, a daily Flying Star number reflects the energy of the day. Understanding the meaning and energy of the Flying Stars allows you to assess the daily quality of luck.

FAVOURABLE STARS

1 Victory Triumph and Success Star **(Water Element):** Helps attain victory over competition and enhances career promotion and monetary growth. Strengthen and improve energy by placing a Victory Horse, Ruyi, or Dragon Tortoise. A water feature would also be incredibly beneficial.

2 Rebirth and Positive Change (Earth Element): This Star supports health growth and well-being, bringing improvement to physical ailments and diseases... Support the energy by placing a Wu Lou (Health Gourd), Six Gold Coins on a red tassel, a Saltwater Cure and a Quan Yin in the Southwest.

4 Romance and Literacy Star (Wood Element): Good Star improves relationship opportunities, study, and literary fortune for writers and scholars. Enhance luck with bright lights, fire energy, and wood energy: Place Mandarin Ducks or Huggers, peach blossom animals, plants and fresh flowers in this area.

6 Heavenly Luck Star (Metal Element): Associated with good fortune and help from heaven, it brings speculative luck, power, and authority. Use bright lights, a water feature and Metal to enhance, such as Six Gold Coins on red tassels and Gold Ingots within this area. A Horse will also assist.

8 Retired Prosperity Star (Earth Element): Signifies steady wealth, prosperity, success and happiness. Strengthen and enhance by placing any form of wealth symbolism such as a Buddha, Wealth God, Six Gold Coins on a red tassel, and Gold Ingots.

9 Multiplying Current Prosperity Star (Fire Element): Signifies future prosperity; spurs celebrations, festivities, gatherings and excellent good luck. Enhance with red accessories, bright lights, or any wealth symbolism such as a Buddha, a Wealth God, 9 Gold Coins on a red tassel, or Gold Ingots.

UNFAVOURABLE STARS

3 Hostile, Conflict and Dispute Star (Wood Element): An evil Star signifies lawsuits, hostility and quarrels. Brings misunderstandings among staff, clients and colleagues and trouble with the authorities. I recommend placing Fire energy in this area, such as bright lights or a red piece of paper, or you can use any red décor object. If your front door is in this area, I recommend placing Temple Lions and the Evil Eye symbol. Remove any excess water or plants. Remove Metal windchimes. Do not overstimulate with radio or TV energy.

5 Misfortune and Obstacles Star (Earth Element), also known as Wu Wang or 5 Yellow Star: It is considered the most vicious and dangerous of the nine Stars; it brings all kinds of misfortunes, accidents, losses and death. Subdue with a Brass 5-element Pagoda and a Saltwater Cure in the centre. A Ganesha will also assist with the removal of obstacles. Keep electrical equipment to a minimum and avoid the colours red and yellow. Try to avoid any significant activity within this sector.

7 Robbery and Evil Star (Metal Element): This unlucky star brings loss, robbery, violence, and gossip to the West sector. Suppress by placing three pieces of Lucky Bamboo in a vase of water and bright lights in this area, along with the Evil Eye

Symbol, one Blue Rhinoceros and one Blue Elephant, or two Blue Rhinoceroses for extra protection. If your front door is located here, I also recommend Temple Lions.

2024 AFFLICTIONS

In 2024, the Southeast (105 - 135) is the designated location of the Tai Sui, also known as the Grand Duke, for the year. The Grand Duke is considered a celestial entity deserving of respect and should not be disturbed or confronted. It is highly recommended to avoid significant renovations or earthmoving in this sector throughout the year and maintain a sense of tranquillity in this area. Placing a Chi Lin, Pi Yao, and Fu Dog in the Southeast, facing the Northwest, can help appease and harmonise this sector, but it's best to avoid disturbances altogether.

Additionally, in 2024, the South is affected by the Three Killings, an energy force associated with health issues and confrontations when disturbed. It's advisable not to have the Three Killings behind you; instead, face this direction. Like the Southeast, it's strongly recommended to refrain from significant renovations or earthmoving in the South and maintain a peaceful environment. Placing blue rectangular rugs and water plants in the South can help mitigate the effects of the Three Killings, but it's preferable not to disturb or renovate this sector in the first place.

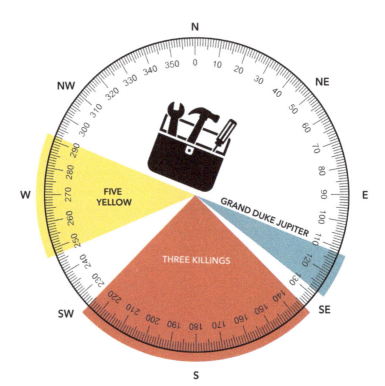

JANUARY 6 – FEBRUARY 3 IS MONTH OF THE OX

OX Chinese Horoscope 2024: Navigating Challenges and Opportunities

(1925, 1937, 1949, 1961, 1973, 1985, 1997, 2009, 2021, 2033)

The Ox in the Chinese zodiac embodies earthy strength, humility, and perseverance, while the Dragon possesses a mystical sky-bound nature. Despite these differences, the Ox and Dragon share a unique synergy in 2024. This alignment hints at potential social difficulties for the Ox in the Year of the Wood Dragon. The year may bring mixed results, posing obstacles in financial and career aspects. However, the Ox can remain hopeful as fortunate stars align, offering unexpected aid.

Renowned for their work ethic and determination, Ox individuals should prioritise harmonious interactions and adhere to responsibilities. Opportunities arise, but pressuring oneself is counterproductive; timing is crucial.

Financial Realm: Prudence and Stability

The Ox Chinese Horoscope 2024 suggests a cautious approach to finances. Refrain from risky investments and meticulously budget expenditures. Lending money to friends or relatives might lead to losses. Focusing on work and delivering consistently can ensure a steady income. Economic sensibilities will guide the Ox toward stability and success, particularly for entrepreneurs who expand their ventures.

Love and Relationships: Flourishing Bonds

In the realm of love, 2024 is a favourable year for the Ox. Strong foundational relationships emerge, often evolving into long-term partnerships. Renowned for loyalty and reliability, the Ox's virtues lead to admiration and trust from partners. Dragon partnerships, in particular, flourish.

Humble flexibility trumps stubbornness and ego. Effective communication fosters harmony and avoids unnecessary conflicts. While Ox men experience more success in finding love, women may need patience to discover lasting partnerships.

Health and Wellness: Striking Emotional Balance

Vigilance against minor ailments caused by stress and overexertion is essential for Ox natives. Emotional vulnerability calls for mindful self-care, meditation, and stress management. Balancing emotions and practicality promotes overall well-being.

Career Prospects 2024: Empowering Growth

The Year of the Wood Dragon holds potential for Ox's career growth and success. Civil Services, Arts, and Media fields offer promotion prospects. Auspicious stars offer empowerment, culminating in recognition and achievements. Collaborative relationships foster guidance and acknowledgment, while challenges and interpersonal issues might arise. Maintain humility and dedication to navigate challenges.

Lucky and Unlucky Aspects: Guiding Forces

Lucky colours (White, Yellow, Green), numbers (1, 4), months (May, February, December), and directions (North, South) favour Ox individuals. Unlucky numbers (5, 6), colour (Blue), and months (April, November) are noted.

Ox and Dragon Synergy: Opportunity and Transformation

The Ox embodies Yin Earth, while the Dragon encompasses Yin Wood and Yin Metal. Their alignment facilitates friendships, financial guidance, and a joyful transformation. The Dragon's influence can empower the Ox to enhance their wealth prospects.

2024: Ox's Journey with the Green Dragon

The Year of the Green Dragon offers the Ox a mix of positive transformations. The Dragon assists the Ox's journey toward prosperity by aiding in wealth accumulation, guiding career development, and enriching social connections.

Balance, Growth, and Transformation

The Wood Dragon Year offers transformative potential as the Ox navigates through challenges and embraces opportunities. Prudent financial strategies, nurturing relationships, and sustaining well-being contribute to a balanced, fulfilling year. Through harmonious collaboration with the Dragon's energy, the Ox's prospects in various aspects are poised for growth and success.

January Flying Star 6, A Radiant Beacon of Authority and Fortune

January starts with the Flying Star 6 stepping into the spotlight as the month's energy. Flying Star 6 is a celestial entity that ushers in a tide of authority, potency, wealth, and the propitious winds of heaven-borne luck. This luminary phenomenon is poised to be the harbinger of prosperous times, orchestrating a grand symphony of career opportunities and the actualisation of long-held aspirations. In its glorious wake, one can anticipate the infusion of enhanced power, elevated stature, and the shimmering aura of a commendable reputation. As an emissary of prosperity, this star graces the scene with divine favour, endowing its beneficiaries with career luck bestowed straight from the heavens. If your gaze falls upon the youngest-born son or the Ox and Tiger in the zodiac realm, know they are poised to reap its bounteous rewards as this star favours their path.

The veneration of this star's positive attributes can lead to the establishment of a commanding presence, indicative of elevated status and influential sway within social circles. The quintessence of authority is encapsulated within its energetic current.

To breathe life into the latent potential of Flying Star 6, one must infuse it with the vigour of Yang energy, invoking the cadence of life through the harmonious interplay of water features, resonant sounds, and vibrant activities. The traditional enhancers echo through time—be it the dignified visage of a Horse figurine, the subtle allure of Six Gold Coins suspended from a tassel, or the enduring emblem of Gold Ingots.

Yet, with all its radiance, it is imperative to tread with caution. Negative external influences can unexpectedly cast a shadow over Flying Star 6, transforming its blessings into turbulent turns. Such unsettling disruptions can manifest as sudden upheavals or abrupt changes, while the spectre of medical complications, particularly about the kidneys or legs, assumes a foreboding presence.

Pertaining to the Luo Shu or Bagua School of Feng Shui, the annual Flying Star 6 sits in the North-East sector for 2024; this sector represents knowledge, scholarly, learning and education.

As the **Northeast** belongs to the element of Earth, this location becomes promising. To support and enhance, use a picture of Mountains, a Crystal Globe, a world map, the Chinese saint Luohan or Dragon Carp. Take note if a large tree or missing space blocks the Northeast sector, as you will need help tapping into learning and knowledge.

01 | JANUARY 2024

The Wood Dragon Year

1 Monday
Animal: **Wood Rat**
Flying Star: **1**
Good Day: **Ox**
Bad Day: **Horse**
🏰

2 Tuesday
Animal: **Wood Ox**
Flying Star: **2**
Good Day: **Rat**
Bad Day: **Goat**
❤️ ✂️ ✈️

3 Wednesday
Animal: **Fire Tiger**
Flying Star: **3**
Good Day: **Pig**
Bad Day: **Monkey**
✂️ ✈️

4 Thursday
Animal: **Fire Rabbit**
Flying Star: **4**
Good Day: **Dog**
Bad Day: **Rooster**

5 Friday
Animal: **Earth Dragon**
Flying Star: **5**
Good Day: **Rooster**
Bad Day: **Dog**
🏰 🏠 ⚡ ✈️

6 Saturday
Animal: **Earth Snake**
Flying Star: **6**
Good Day: **Monkey**
Bad Day: **Pig**
🏰 🏠 ❤️

7 Sunday
Animal: **Metal Horse**
Flying Star: **7**
Good Day: **Goat**
Bad Day: **Rat**
🏰 ❤️ ✈️

JANUARY MONTHLY CHINESE ZODIAC OVERVIEW

Rat, After a busy and rewarding year, it is time to reflect on your experiences and set new intentions for 2024. For now, upholding strong business ethics will enhance your decision-making. As you enter a brand-new Lunar Year, you must prioritise rest and wellness to recharge your energies.

Ox The year has been a blend of intriguing experiences, often upbeat, with a few tumultuous months. You can confidently enter the new Lunar Year with lessons from overcoming challenges. It is a busy work month, but you must try to soak in the current vibrant energy and recharge your batteries.

Tiger As the Rabbit year draws to a close, there is still work to be accomplished. This month presents abundant and harmonious energy that you can embrace and relish. Additionally, it is an opportune time to focus on optimising your well-being and ensuring you are revitalised for the upcoming Lunar Year.

Rabbit This month's energy will elevate your physical and emotional well-being. As you embrace the positive energy ushered in by the new Lunar Year, be prepared for a surge in your activities. This period presents a golden opportunity to indulge in self-care and rejuvenation, enabling you to be fully recharged and revitalised.

Dragon While the Rabbit year has its stresses, many of you would have navigated through it with strength and determination. It is time to set new intentions for yet another brand-new Lunar Year. Prioritising your well-being and maintaining a positive outlook continue to be crucial. Many aspects of your life in 2024 indicate positive shifts and changes.

Snake The past year may have been exhausting, but it has brought its rewards. As you enter another brand-new Lunar Year, anxieties will dissipate, leading you to a more contented state. Self-care is a priority right now; indulging in well-deserved pampering, gatherings, outdoor activities, and spa treats is essential. If you are involved in business, it is best to avoid impulsive decisions to prevent potential losses

Horse As the Rabbit year draws to a close, it is essential to reflect on your journey. As you step into the energy of the new Lunar Year, you will be filled with new possibilities and optimism. It is also an ideal time to set your sights on your goals and financial plans for the upcoming year. Taking time out to recharge your energy is also vital during this time.

Goat As you transition into a new Lunar Year, it is essential to take time out for self-care and introspection. Dedicate this month to yourself by indulging in activities that bring you peace and relaxation.

01 | JANUARY 2024

The Wood Dragon Year

8 Monday
Animal: **Metal Goat**
Flying Star: **8**
Good Day: **Ox**
Bad Day: **Rat**

9 Tuesday
Animal: **Water Monkey**
Flying Star: **9**
Good Day: **Snake**
Bad Day: **Tiger**
❤ ✈

10 Wednesday
Animal: **Water Rooster**
Flying Star: **1**
Good Day: **Dragon**
Bad Day: **Rabbit**

11 Thursday
Animal: **Wood Dog**
Flying Star: **2**
Good Day: **Rabbit**
Bad Day: **Draon**
❤ ⚡

12 Friday
Animal: **Wood Pig**
Flying Star: **3**
Good Day: **Tiger**
Bad Day: **Snake**
⚡ ✈

13 Saturday
Animal: **Fire Rat**
Flying Star: **4**
Good Day: **Ox**
Bad Day: **Horse**

14 Sunday
Animal: **Fire Ox**
Flying Star: **5**
Good Day: **Rat**
Bad Day: **Goat**
⚡

Monkey As you step into the new Lunar Year, mentally preparing for further transformations on the horizon is essential. Be ready to embrace adjustments and shifts as they come. Travel opportunities will likely arise, and you might even receive news of potential work in a different location. Be open to new experiences and possibilities as you navigate these changes.

Rooster The Year of the Rabbit, has challenged you and provided numerous avenues for personal growth that have shaped your journey meaningfully. For now, it is an excellent time to set aside some time to review your plans and goals.

Dog Overall, your journey in 2024 might have been uncomfortable, but it will be a catalyst for your personal growth. As you enter the new Lunar Year, you will find more harmony and rewards. Embrace the bright and optimistic energy with enthusiasm and confidence, knowing that your experiences have prepared you for a more colourful and fulfilling journey in 2024.

Pig The energy is dynamic, and things will continue to flow smoothly for you. You will feel confident and happy with your past year's achievements. As we approach the next Lunar Year, we must set new goals and visions. You will benefit from an evenly paced lifestyle and focus on enhancing personal wellness.

01 | JANUARY 2024

The Wood Dragon Year

15 Monday
Animal: **Earth Tiger**
Flying Star: **6**
Good Day: **Pig**
Bad Day: **Monkey**
🏭🏠🔪

16 Tuesday
Animal: **Earth Rabbit**
Flying Star: **7**
Good Day: **Dog**
Bad Day: **Rooster**
❤️🔪

17 Wednesday
Animal: **Metal Dragon**
Flying Star: **8**
Good Day: **Rooster**
Bad Day: **Dog**

18 Thursday
Animal: **Metal Snake**
Flying Star: **9**
Good Day: **Monkey**
Bad Day: **Pig**
🏭❤️

19 Friday
Animal: **Water Horse**
Flying Star: **1**
Good Day: **Goat**
Bad Day: **Rat**
🏭🏠❤️

20 Saturday
Animal: **Water Goat**
Flying Star: **2**
Good Day: **Horse**
Bad Day: **Ox**

21 Sunday
Animal: **Wood Monkey**
Flying Star: **3**
Good Day: **Snake**
Bad Day: **Tiger**
🏭🏠❤️🔪✈️

THE FENG SHUI OF YOUR FRONT DOOR

The significance of the main entrance cannot be overstated, as it serves as the gateway for chi, the vital life force energy, to enter your home. The condition of the chi surrounding your front door can influence the energy within, impacting the well-being of all occupants. Assessing and enhancing the feng shui of your main door is a pivotal step in fostering positive energy flow.

Eliminate any potential 'poison arrows' directed at your main door. Be vigilant for sharp edges and triangular rooflines pointing towards the entrance. If feasible, consider relocating the main door to a more favourable position to avoid negative energy influences.

Avoid positioning the main door beneath a bathroom. If this configuration exists, consider moving the entrance to a different area along the frontage to mitigate any adverse effects.

Ensure that the main door does not directly face narrow gaps between buildings. Such an alignment may lead to health issues and financial setbacks. Opt for a relocation if necessary.

Keep the area around the main door clean and unobstructed. Avoid placing shoes directly before the entrance to maintain a smooth, positive energy flow.

Allow some open space in front of the main door to facilitate the pooling and gentle energy flow into your home. This practice is believed to attract good luck and positive vibes.

Ensure the main door is proportionate to the size of your house. A considerable door may contribute to financial challenges, while a door that is too small can disrupt familial harmony. Strive for a balanced and harmonious entrance that complements the overall scale of your home.

01 | JANUARY 2024

The Wood Dragon Year

22 Monday
Animal: **Wood Rooster**
Flying Star: **4**
Good Day: **Dragon**
Bad Day: **Rabbit**

23 Tuesday
Animal: **Wood Dog**
Flying Star: **5**
Good Day: **Rabbit**
Bad Day: **Dragon**

24 Wednesday
Animal: **Fire Pig**
Flying Star: **6**
Good Day: **Tiger**
Bad Day: **Snake**

25 Thursday
Animal: **Fire Rat**
Flying Star: **7**
Good Day: **Ox**
Bad Day: **Horse**

26 Friday
Animal: **Earth Ox**
Flying Star: **8**
Good Day: **Rat**
Bad Day: **Goat**

27 Saturday
Animal: **Earth Tiger**
Flying Star: **9**
Good Day: **Pig**
Bad Day: **Monkey**

28 Sunday
Animal: **Metal Rabbit**
Flying Star: **1**
Good Day: **Dog**
Bad Day: **Rooster**

01 | JANUARY 2024

The Wood Dragon Year

29 Monday
Animal: **Metal Dragon**
Flying Star: **2**
Good Day: **Rooster**
Bad Day: **Dog**

30 Tuesday
Animal: **Water Snake**
Flying Star: **3**
Good Day: **Monkey**
Bad Day: **Pig**
🎬🏠❤️

31 Wednesday
Animal: **Water Horse**
Flying Star: **4**
Good Day: **Goat**
Bad Day: **Rat**
🎬🏠❤️✈️

1 Thursday
Animal: **Wood Goat**
Flying Star: **5**
Good Day: **Horse**
Bad Day: **Ox**
⚡

2 Friday
Animal: **Fire Monkey**
Flying Star: **6**
Good Day: **Snake**
Bad Day: **Tiger**
❤️🏠✂️🎬

3 Saturday
Animal: **Fire Rooster**
Flying Star: **7**
Good Day: **Dragon**
Bad Day: **Rabbit**
🎬

4 Sunday
Animal: **Earth Dog**
Flying Star: **8**
Good Day: **Rabbit**
Bad Day: **Dragon**
⚡🎬

FEBRUARY 4 – MARCH 5 IS MONTH OF THE TIGER

TIGER Chinese Horoscope 2024: Navigating Challenges and Prosperity

(1926, 1938, 1950, 1962, 1974, 1986, 1998, 2010, 2022, 2034)

The Tiger zodiac, linked with the Wood element, faces a contrasting year alongside the Earth-connected Dragon. This signifies a dynamic and demanding 2024. Given the conflicting relationship between Wood and Fire elements, maintaining tranquillity and avoiding disputes is crucial for the Tiger to thrive in the Year of the Wood Dragon.

Financial Outlook: Caution and Vigilance

The Tiger's financial journey in 2024 is marked by fluctuations, necessitating cautious navigation. Steer clear of risky economic ventures. While business travel is on the horizon, prioritise safety and well-being.

Career Challenges and Resilience

Tigers will encounter career obstacles in 2024. Even without errors, challenges are likely. Remaining composed and wise while adhering to regulations will help. Avoid disagreements with colleagues or clients, safeguarding career progression. Prepare for unforeseen events by preserving energy and resources.

Career Progress and Artistic Fields

Tigers aligning with the Wood element, especially those in creative domains like arts and culture, will find career opportunities. Skill display and job prospects will be abundant in these fields.

Mixed Love Fortunes: Patience and Communication

Love experiences for Tigers in 2024 exhibit variability. Single Tigers will meet potential partners, but prudent, gradual steps are advised. Committed Tigers may face miscommunications; open dialogue and patience mend these. Married Tigers can ensure stability by nurturing their relationships with shared activities and vacations.

Positive Career Prospects: Empowerment and Humility

Tiger's career outlook in the Year of the Wood Dragon is promising. Tigers' diligent and dedicated traits yield novel career prospects. Recognition and appreciation elevate reputation. Humility complements success, ensuring a balanced approach.

Favourable Finance Opportunities: Planning and Restraint

Financially, Tigers possess determination and hard work. Proper planning and fiscal discipline promote growth and stability. Reserve funds safeguard against unexpected expenses. Impulsive spending should be avoided in love, career, or finances.

Holistic Health: Routine and Well-being

A disciplined routine, daily exercise, and mindfulness practices ensure Tiger's well-being. Managing stress through meditation, Pranayama, Yoga, or Tai Chi fosters mental and physical health. Vigilance against tobacco and smoking aligns with Tiger's determination and strength.

Dragon and Tiger Harmony: Mutual Benefit

The Tiger embodies Yang Wood, while the Dragon symbolises Yang Earth and Yin Water. This synergy fuels prosperity and career growth. Tigers act as business leaders, and Dragon supports wealth accumulation, creating a harmonious partnership.

2024: The Power of Tiger and Dragon

The conjunction of Tiger and Dragon ushers in a year of opportunity and transformation. Tigers will triumph by embracing challenges and capitalising on their inherent traits.

Balancing Elements: Collaboration and Prosperity

As Tiger and Dragon collaborate, they amplify each other's strengths. Tigers' diplomatic prowess aligns with Dragon's internal management skills, facilitating success and wealth accumulation.

Embracing Wealth: Unity and Prosperity

The Year of the Wood Dragon bestows Tigers with a remarkable blend of power and affluence. Tigers' drive and resilience converge with Dragon's guidance, leading to financial prosperity.

Navigating Relationships: Communication and Harmony

Misunderstandings and conflicts may impact love and relationships. Effective communication and mutual respect are the keys to resolving disputes. Committed Tigers thrive through shared activities and quality time.

In Pursuit of Career: Dedication and Triumph

Tigers' diligence and dedication result in career accomplishments. Humility and adherence to rules accompany success. Novel opportunities, recognition, and progress shape Tiger's professional journey.

Financial Advancement: Planning and Progress

Tigers achieve financial stability through prudent planning and fiscal restraint. Vigilance against impulsive spending and strategic investments foster economic growth.

Wellness and Vitality: Mindfulness and Balance

Health rests on disciplined routines, daily exercise, and mindfulness practices. Stress management and healthy habits yield holistic well-being. Strong willpower, symbolising the Tiger, ensures sound mental and physical health.

Dragon and Tiger Synergy: Prosperity and Success

The conjunction of Tiger and Dragon symbolises a year of advancement and transformation. Collaborating harmoniously, they unlock opportunities and surmount challenges, propelling Tigers toward a year of achievement.

FEBRUARY Flying Star 5, A Star of Dark Omens and Harbingers of Misfortune

February finds the energy of the Flying Star 5 taking centre stage, entering into the intricate tapestry of cosmic powers. The ominous presence of Flying Star 5, commonly recognised as the difficult 5 Yellow Star, casts its malevolent shadow. This harbinger of danger, misfortune, and an array of disorders stands as one of the most treacherous and aggressive celestial phenomena within the realm of Feng Shui. Its reputation precedes it—a harbinger of woes, a herald of bad luck, an orchestrator of obstacles, a weaver of calamities, and a conductor of misadventures.

As its ominous energy unfurls, it weaves a web of adversity and hindrances, casting its baleful influence overall in its wake. This maleficent star exudes a toxic aura that magnetises unfavourable outcomes, particularly inauspicious for the youngest daughter and those born under the Rooster sign. Its pernicious effects are vast and disheartening—ranging from financial loss, business disruption, and betrayals to more dire manifestations like tragic accidents, grave injuries, and even fatal calamities.

A lurking sense of trepidation surrounds the Flying Star 5, as it embodies an array of negative energies that can envelop one's endeavours in a shroud of despair. It is the embodiment of bankruptcy, disloyalty, betrayals, and other harbingers of doom that threaten to overturn even the most stable foundations.

To shield against its ominous grasp, the ancient wisdom of Feng Shui imparts sage advice. Breaking ground or embarking on new renovation projects during the presence of this star is ill-advised, as it may unleash its potent negativity. The most powerful method of managing its influence lies in non-interference—let it lie dormant and undisturbed as much as possible. However, for situations where avoidance isn't feasible, one may seek solace in remedies like the Brass Pagoda, the sombre notes of the Bonze bell, the harmonious melody of metal wind chimes, and the purifying Saltwater Cure. The benevolent presence of Ganesha, the remover of obstacles, can also be invoked to mitigate its dire effects.

To counteract the grip of this adversarial star, heavy metal objects crafted from brass, copper, bronze, or pewter can be strategically placed at the heart of one's abode—the Centre. Radiating metallic artwork, hues, and home décor items can echo the sentiment of resistance against its influences, while measures to minimise Fire and Earth energies diminish its potency.

Pertaining to the Luo Shu or Bagua school of Feng Shui, the annual Flying Star 5 sits in the West sector for 2024; this sector is representative of descendants, family and children luck, and the protection of your current assets and wealth.

The **Western** sector is the home of the celestial white Tiger, so placing the symbolism of the Tiger in the West can protect the family's luck. Place any wealth symbolism in the western area to assist protection and for the family to remain healthy and strong together. The West belongs to the element of Metal. For 2024, enhance wealth luck with Gold Coins, Gold Ingots, a Wealth God, metallic artwork, paintings or colours. The West wall is a favourable position for family photos in metallic frames.

02 | FEBRUARY 2024

The Wood Dragon Year

5 Monday
Animal: **Earth Pig**
Flying Star: **9**
Good Day: **Tiger**
Bad Day: **Snake**

6 Tuesday
Animal: **Metal Rat**
Flying Star: **1**
Good Day: **Ox**
Bad Day: **Horse**

7 Wednesday
Animal: **Metal Ox**
Flying Star: **2**
Good Day: **Rat**
Bad Day: **Goat**

8 Thursday
Animal: **Water Tiger**
Flying Star: **3**
Good Day: **Pig**
Bad Day: **Monkey**

9 Friday
Animal: **Water Rabbit**
Flying Star: **4**
Good Day: **Dog**
Bad Day: **Rooster**

10 Saturday
Animal: **Wood Dragon**
Flying Star: **5**
Good Day: **Rooster**
Bad Day: **Dog**

11 Sunday
Animal: **Wood Snake**
Flying Star: **6**
Good Day: **Monkey**
Bad Day: **Pig**

FEBRUARY MONTHLY CHINESE ZODIAC OVERVIEW

Rat February is a favourable month for those born under the Rat Sign. You will feel energised and optimistic generally, but beware that on the flip side is the sense of heightened sensitivity and susceptibility to agitation. Although fresh energy fuels your drive to progress, this period is not ideal for significant change.

Ox The high and positive energy at the start of the month will enhance your physical and mental self. It is essential to take full advantage of this time. In a business or work environment, you will have a smoother time if you can keep steadfast, steer clear of conflicts and refrain from impulsive choices.

Tiger In your professional life, doing more planning and research before presenting proposals is essential. Job seekers are likely to find opportunities. It is crucial to overcome feelings of being unappreciated, as these will get you down. It is recommended to postpone significant decisions until the following month.

Rabbit Business and financial prospects hold a positive outlook, potentially leading to increased profits or income. However, work demands might intensify towards the latter part of the month. Caution is needed when dealing with documents, as indications of errors are present. Be exceptionally vigilant if signing contracts during this period.

Dragon Setting a solid intention to be optimistic this month is vital as February is demanding. It is essential to allow time for the energy of the new Lunar Year to set in. Take note that financial matters will take a longer time to balance out. Exercise and outdoor activities will help to reduce your stress.

Snake In this month, the energy focuses mainly on your transformation. You must tap into your inner strength and recognise your capabilities before initiating positive shifts. When dealing with work or business matters, one must be aware of boundaries that shouldn't be crossed.

Horse This is a creative month, and it will be easier to manage productivity at work. However, you should maintain a balanced approach to actions and decisions. During this time, it is also crucial to exercise caution when dealing with financial matters; avoiding risks and impulsive choices can safeguard your financial stability.

Goat The energy of this month encourages you to reflect on your vision and aspirations for the year. Using this time to channel your energy towards accomplishing your goals and avoid excessive worrying is wise. Remember that maintaining emotional balance is critical to navigating through this month effectively.

02 | FEBRUARY 2024

The Wood Dragon Year

12 Monday
Animal: **Fire Horse**
Flying Star: **7**
Good Day: **Goat**
Bad Day: **Rat**

13 Tuesday
Animal: **Fire Goat**
Flying Star: **8**
Good Day: **Horse**
Bad Day: **Ox**
✈️❤️🏠🎬

14 Wednesday
Animal: **Earth Monkey**
Flying Star: **9**
Good Day: **Snake**
Bad Day: **Tiger**

15 Thursday
Animal: **Earth Rooster**
Flying Star: **1**
Good Day: **Dragon**
Bad Day: **Rabbit**
✈️🏠🎬

16 Friday
Animal: **Metal Dog**
Flying Star: **2**
Good Day: **Rabbit**
Bad Day: **Dragon**
⚡🎬

17 Saturday
Animal: **Metal Pig**
Flying Star: **3**
Good Day: **Tiger**
Bad Day: **Snake**
✈️🏠🎬

18 Sunday
Animal: **Water Rat**
Flying Star: **4**
Good Day: **Ox**
Bad Day: **Horse**
❤️🎬

Monkey The beginning of the Dragon year brings you stable and supportive energy. It is an excellent time to reassess your goals and ensure they align with your passions and desires. If you plan to travel this month, expect a peaceful and enjoyable journey. You will feel a sense of peace and satisfaction, allowing you to start the year positively.

Rooster As you approach the Yang Wood Dragon energy, it is essential to mentally prepare for transformations and be ready to accept adjustments and shifts. This is an excellent time to focus on your passions, love, and aspirations in all aspects of your life. If your current pursuits oppose your desires, it is time to reconsider your choices.

Dog February begins with highly positive energy that enables smoother transitions for contracts and negotiations. New tasks and opportunities are indicated. Be aware of competition at your workplace and that some of your ideas may face initial resistance from others. Though money matters seem optimistic, vigilance is still needed. With a prudent approach, you can make the most of the start of this auspicious and festive season.

Pig The year begins with supportive energy for your zodiac. Your power will be significantly enhanced, and all good things can happen. There is great potential for work achievements that will bring rewards and fulfilment. This is a good money month, and extra income is indicated. Embrace the positive momentum and enjoy yourself.

02 | FEBRUARY 2024

The Wood Dragon Year

19 Monday
Animal: **Wood Ox**
Flying Star: **5**
Good Day: **Rat**
Bad Day: **Goat**
⚡

20 Tuesday
Animal: **Fire Tiger**
Flying Star: **6**
Good Day: **Pig**
Bad Day: **Monkey**
✏️💼

21 Wednesday
Animal: **Fire Rabbit**
Flying Star: **7**
Good Day: **Dog**
Bad Day: **Rooster**
✏️✈️❤️🏠

22 Thursday
Animal: **Earth Dragon**
Flying Star: **8**
Good Day: **Rooster**
Bad Day: **Dog**
✈️❤️

23 Friday
Animal: **Earth Snake**
Flying Star: **9**
Good Day: **Monkey**
Bad Day: **Pig**

24 Saturday
Animal: **Metal Horse**
Flying Star: **1**
Good Day: **Goat**
Bad Day: **Rat**
✏️✈️🏠

25 Sunday
Animal: **Metal Goat**
Flying Star: **2**
Good Day: **Horse**
Bad Day: **Ox**
❤️💼

02 | FEBRUARY 2024

The Wood Dragon Year

26 Monday
Animal: **Water Monkey**
Flying Star: **3**
Good Day: **Snake**
Bad Day: **Tiger**

27 Tuesday
Animal: **Water Rooster**
Flying Star: **4**
Good Day: **Dragon**
Bad Day: **Rabbit**
🎬

28 Wednesday
Animal: **Wood Dog**
Flying Star: **5**
Good Day: **Rabbit**
Bad Day: **Dragon**
⚡🏰

29 Thursday
Animal: **Wood Pig**
Flying Star: **6**
Good Day: **Tiger**
Bad Day: **Snake**

1 Friday
Animal: **Wood Rat**
Flying Star: **7**
Good Day: **Ox**
Bad Day: **Horse**
✂️✈️❤️🏰

2 Saturday
Animal: **Wood Ox**
Flying Star: **8**
Good Day: **Rat**
Bad Day: **Goat**

3 Sunday
Animal: **Fire Tiger**
Flying Star: **9**
Good Day: **Pig**
Bad Day: **Monkey**
✂️

MARCH 6 – APRIL 4 IS THE MONTH OF THE RABBIT

RABBIT Chinese Horoscope 2024: Challenges and Prosperity Ahead

(1915, 1927, 1939, 1951, 1963, 1975, 1987, 1999, 2011, 2023, 2035)

Rabbits are known for their artistic inclinations and appreciation of nature's beauty. With a thoughtful and observant nature, they excel as mediators and diplomats. Their loyalty and romance make them stand out.

Rabbit-Dragon Dynamic: Harmony and Tensions

In 2024, the Rabbit and Dragon coexist with shared traits but distinct challenges. Rabbit carries the Wood element, while Dragon is Earth-aligned. This parallel connection introduces complexities to family life, leading to potential disputes.

However, Rabbits find solace in the Sun star's support, offering help in times of trouble. Relationships, both social and business, prosper due to Rabbit-Dragon's proximity.

Career Outlook: Opportunities and Hurdles

Career luck favours Rabbits in 2024. Yet, envious individuals pose obstacles. Rabbits should sidestep conflicts, focus on a steady income, and avoid lending to relatives to evade legal issues.

Love Prospects: Progress and Communication

Rabbits encounter romantic hurdles in 2024 due to the Rabbit-Dragon separation. Gradual steps and clear communication foster successful love journeys. Singles can find soulmates, but patience is vital. Committed Rabbits nurture partnerships through mutual respect.

Career Growth: Skill Enhancement and Collaboration

The Year of the Wood Dragon brings mixed career results. Rabbits must hone skills and undertake professional development courses. Collaborating with colleagues, despite the rivalry, aids career growth. Focus on April, August, and December for career advancement.

Financial Gains: Caution and Wealth

Rabbits enjoy financial prosperity in 2024. However, Dragon's volatility demands careful research before investing. Balance rationality and business acumen to maximise wealth opportunities.

Wellness and Harmony: Mind and Body Balance

Health thrives for Rabbits in 2024, but emotional health is paramount. Manage stress through exercise, meditation, and balanced routines. Careful attention to well-being and timely medical consultation ensures vitality.

Rabbit and Dragon Partnership: Prosperity and Unity

Rabbits and Dragons blend strengths harmoniously, amplifying career and financial prospects. Grass slowly covering mountains symbolises Rabbits' persistent efforts leading to abundant wealth.

Holistic Prosperity: Growth and Cautious Investment

Rabbits encounter financial opportunities in the Year of the Wood Dragon. Cautious investments in robust sectors secure prosperity. Balance rationality and caution for optimal results.

Health and Vitality: Nurturing Mind and Body

Physical and emotional health benefits from Rabbit-Dragon synergy. Maintain well-being through exercise, meditation, and discipline. Staying mindful prevents health issues and supports overall vitality.

Rabbit and Dragon Unity: Achievement and Triumph

The Rabbit's artistic sensibilities blend with the Dragon's majestic qualities. Collaboration heralds a year of triumph marked by successes and opportunities.

Dragon and Rabbit Compatibility: Growth and Harmony

The Dragon's Earth enhances the Rabbit's wealth, while the Rabbit's Wood fuels the Dragon's career. Harmonious collaboration ensures mutual success.

Chinese Zodiac Rabbit: Challenges and Success

The Rabbit thrives in the Year of the Wood Dragon. Challenges exist, but diligent efforts bring growth and achievement.

2024: Rabbit and Dragon Synergy

Collaboration between the Rabbit and Dragon leads to success and transformation. Navigate challenges, seize opportunities, and attain prosperous outcomes.

MARCH Flying Star 4, Romance, Wisdom, and Scholarly Flourish

March's monthly energy is of romance, wisdom, and a scholarly flourish, with the Flying Star 4 emerging as a harmonious melody that resonates with a tapestry of attributes within the cosmic symphony of celestial energies. It brings romance, intelligence, talent, and wisdom, weaving threads of fame, promotion, and academic brilliance into the fabric of existence. Often referred to as the Peach Blossom Star, it exudes an aura of beauty, knowledge, and learning that enriches the lives it touches.

As the energies of Flying Star 4 infuse the surroundings, an enchanting dance of harmony and happiness envelops love relationships. Its benevolent influence sets the stage for meaningful and fulfilling connections, making it especially promising for singles seeking the blossoming of love and marriage. This star's tender touch fosters an environment where the seeds of romance can flourish, yielding companionship and a profound depth of emotion.

Beyond matters of the heart, Flying Star 4 bestows its blessings upon individuals with a literary, artistic, or creative inclination. For educators, lecturers, artists, writers, and researchers, its presence brings positive outcomes, hinting at the promise of advancement and recognition. Students, too, are enveloped by its embrace, with better luck in examinations and increased success in applications for esteemed educational institutions.

To nurture the flames of love and romance, couples are urged to adorn their spaces with symbols of affection. Placing two Rose Quartz crystals near or beneath the bed is a beacon of love's energy. Love symbols such as Mandarin Ducks, Wish-fulfilling Birds, or embracing figurines are tangible reminders of the shared tender connection.

For those seeking to amplify their academic fortunes, Flying Star 4 beckons them to embrace the scholarly realm. The display of Chinese ink brushes or artistic renderings, tiered pagodas, revered Chinese saint Luohan, or the revered three Star Gods can harmoniously intertwine with this star's essence. Through these tokens, the path to academic excellence finds itself illuminated by the benevolent glow of Flying Star 4.

Pertaining to the Luo Shu or Bagua school of Feng Shui, the annual Flying Star 4 sits in the North-West sector for 2024; this sector represents the man of the house and signifies influential benefactors, mentors, and helpful people.

The **North West** belongs to the element of Metal; in Chinese culture, metal also signifies gold. So, this is also a pocket of family wealth. To tap into and enhance, use metal décor items, coloured objects, bells or wind chimes. The three Star Gods represent health, wealth and longevity and are excellent used in a home's main living area to benefit all occupants.

03 | MARCH 2024

The Wood Dragon Year

4 Monday
Animal: **Fire Rabbit**
Flying Star: **1**
Good Day: **Dog**
Bad Day: **Rooster**
✈️ ❤️ 🎰

5 Tuesday
Animal: **Earth Dragon**
Flying Star: **2**
Good Day: **Rooster**
Bad Day: **Dog**

6 Wednesday
Animal: **Earth Snake**
Flying Star: **3**
Good Day: **Monkey**
Bad Day: **Pig**

7 Thursday
Animal: **Metal Horse**
Flying Star: **4**
Good Day: **Goat**
Bad Day: **Rat**

8 Friday
Animal: **Metal Goat**
Flying Star: **5**
Good Day: **Horse**
Bad Day: **Ox**
⚡ ❤️

9 Saturday
Animal: **Water Monkey**
Flying Star: **6**
Good Day: **Snake**
Bad Day: **Tiger**
🎰

10 Sunday
Animal: **Water Rooster**
Flying Star: **7**
Good Day: **Dragon**
Bad Day: **Rabbit**

2024 Feng Shui and Chinese Astrology Planner

MARCH MONTHLY CHINESE ZODIAC OVERVIEW

Rat While this month's energy can be unsettling for some, it is still productive. Manage change carefully at work, especially if there are disagreements between co-workers. Financially, exercise prudence as this might not be a suitable time for substantial risk-taking.

Ox Achieving the success that you desire will require time. Cultivating a positive and considerate mindset when collaborating with others is essential this month. Set realistic expectations for both you and your co-workers. To enhance your well-being, ensure a balance between your activities and your lifestyle.

Tiger This month carries a surge of energy that can affect your emotions. Plans might undergo several alterations before finding their proper alignment. Regarding work decisions, rely on your inner guidance and stand your ground as others might not share your perspective.

Rabbit This month's energy will trigger shifts and transformations. You might experience a sense of unease, especially in your work environment. To navigate this, try focusing on the broader perspective and be adaptable. Maintaining a healthy distance from co-workers is advised for the time being.

Dragon The energy this month continues to be solid and competitive. If you hold a position of authority in your workplace, practising fairness and impartiality when interacting with subordinates and colleagues is crucial. While your financial prospects are positive, you are cautioned to take more care with personal belongings, especially if you are travelling this month.

Snake Be aware and moderate your expectations, as the slow energy of this month might hinder your progress. Business partnerships could also encounter challenges. By addressing matters openly, you can work towards improving your connections and resolve any lingering issues.

Horse This month requires more insight than hard work. It is important to note that simply working hard is not enough for you to achieve your desired goals. To help yourself, you must stay attuned to the evolving world around you, be adaptable and open to making necessary adjustments as the situation requires.

Goat The energy of this month can be intense and may challenge your ideals and aspirations. Finding moments of quiet reflection is essential to recharge your energy and regain focus. Trust in your abilities and have confidence in decision-making.

03 | MARCH 2024

The Wood Dragon Year

11 Monday
Animal: **Wood Dog**
Flying Star: **8**
Good Day: **Rabbit**
Bad Day: **Dragon**
✈️ ❤️ 🏠 ⚡ 🎬

12 Tuesday
Animal: **Wood Pig**
Flying Star: **9**
Good Day: **Tiger**
Bad Day: **Snake**
✈️ 🏠 ✏️ 🎬

13 Wednesday
Animal: **Fire Rat**
Flying Star: **1**
Good Day: **Ox**
Bad Day: **Horse**
❤️

14 Thursday
Animal: **Fire Ox**
Flying Star: **2**
Good Day: **Rat**
Bad Day: **Goat**
✈️ 🎬

15 Friday
Animal: **Earth Tiger**
Flying Star: **3**
Good Day: **Pig**
Bad Day: **Monkey**
✏️ 🎬

16 Saturday
Animal: **Earth Rabbit**
Flying Star: **4**
Good Day: **Dog**
Bad Day: **Rooster**
✈️ ❤️

17 Sunday
Animal: **Metal Dragon**
Flying Star: **5**
Good Day: **Rooster**
Bad Day: **Dog**
⚡

Monkey This month encourages you to delve into your ideals and passions and cultivate a deeper connection with your inner self. Through this process of self-discovery, you will uncover new insights and perspectives that will help you shape a life that truly resonates with your authentic self.

Rooster This month's energy highlights the potential for new beginnings. Spend some time to define your goals for the near future clearly. When it comes to business decisions, be aware that choices made now will have a lasting impact. You might be called upon to extend a helping hand to those who might be facing challenges.

Dog You may encounter some obstacles that may make you feel trapped. Please take note that it might be tough to implement changes during this period. To help yourself, you must maintain a positive mindset and be more flexible. On a brighter note, social life and health are expected to improve.

Pig The energy of this month is optimistic, and life will flow harmoniously. Work energy remains stable, but is not the ideal time for significant changes. Relax and make the most of this favourable time. Money energy is average, so manage finances wisely. Relaxation and social activities are essential.

03 | MARCH 2024

The Wood Dragon Year

18 Monday
Animal: **Metal Snake**
Flying Star: **6**
Good Day: **Monkey**
Bad Day: **Pig**

19 Tuesday
Animal: **Water Horse**
Flying Star: **7**
Good Day: **Goat**
Bad Day: **Rat**

20 Wednesday
Animal: **Water Goat**
Flying Star: **8**
Good Day: **Horse**
Bad Day: **Ox**

21 Thursday
Animal: **Water Monkey**
Flying Star: **9**
Good Day: **Snake**
Bad Day: **Tiger**

22 Friday
Animal: **Wood Rooster**
Flying Star: **1**
Good Day: **Dragon**
Bad Day: **Rabbit**

23 Saturday
Animal: **Wood Dog**
Flying Star: **2**
Good Day: **Rabbit**
Bad Day: **Dragon**

24 Sunday
Animal: **Fire Pig**
Flying Star: **3**
Good Day: **Tiger**
Bad Day: **Snake**

2024 Feng Shui and Chinese Astrology Planner

03 | MARCH 2024

The Wood Dragon Year

25 Monday
Animal: **Fire Rat**
Flying Star: **4**
Good Day: **Ox**
Bad Day: **Horse**
❤️

26 Tuesday
Animal: **Earth Ox**
Flying Star: **5**
Good Day: **Rat**
Bad Day: **Goat**
⚡❤️🏠🎬

27 Wednesday
Animal: **Earth Tiger**
Flying Star: **6**
Good Day: **Pig**
Bad Day: **Monkey**
✏️🎬

28 Thursday
Animal: **Metal Rabbit**
Flying Star: **7**
Good Day: **Dog**
Bad Day: **Rooster**
✈️❤️

29 Friday
Animal: **Metal Dragon**
Flying Star: **8**
Good Day: **Rooster**
Bad Day: **Dog**

30 Saturday
Animal: **Water Snake**
Flying Star: **9**
Good Day: **Monkey**
Bad Day: **Pig**
✏️

31 Sunday
Animal: **Water Horse**
Flying Star: **1**
Good Day: **Goat**
Bad Day: **Rat**
❤️

APRIL 5 – MAY 5 IS MONTH OF THE DRAGON

DRAGON Chinese Horoscope 2024: The Year of Growth and Power

(1916, 1928, 1940, 1952, 1964, 1976, 1988, 2000, 2012, 2024, 2036)

The Year 2024 is marked by Wood for the Dragon, making it the Year of the Wood Dragon. Wood signifies growth, success, and the initial stages of development. This year brings new beginnings, hard work, and potential prosperity.

Dragon's Elemental Influence: Wood and Fire

Connected to Wood, the Dragon of 2024 embodies growth, innovation, and creativity. Wood's relationship with Fire creates passion, invention, and transformation. This partnership ignites a spark that can evolve into a significant event.

The Green Energy of Growth

Symbolised by the colour green, Wood stands for vitality and life. Like plants needing care to flourish, individuals must nourish their bodies, minds, and souls to achieve prosperity and wisdom. This year energises personal, professional, and spiritual growth.

Harnessing Power with Humility

While abundant opportunities arise, Dragons must remain humble and grounded. Balancing ambition with humility will allow them to harness the powerful energy for enduring success.

Dragon Love Horoscope 2024: Prosperity and Challenges

The Year of the Wood Dragon brings fortune and abundance for love. Strengthening existing relationships and fostering family bonds are highlighted. Singles can expect new connections, and those planning a family can benefit from Dragon's fertility energy.

Dragon Career Horoscope 2024: Innovation and Growth

The Year of the Wood Dragon encourages innovation, creation, and calculated risks in careers. Stepping out of comfort zones, turning passions into professions, and embracing change lead to unexpected growth. Sectors like technology and renewable energy thrive, aligning with Wood's influence.

Dragon Finance Horoscope 2024: Opportunities and Caution

Numerous financial opportunities emerge in 2024. Investments in robust sectors yield high returns, particularly in technology, renewable energy, electronics, and insurance. Careful research is advised before making financial decisions.

Dragon Health Horoscope 2024: Balancing Ambition and Health

Hardworking Dragons should prioritise health. Adequate sleep, daily exercise, meditation, and a balanced lifestyle are essential. The Year of the Wood Dragon brings vitality, but maintaining physical and mental well-being is crucial to harnessing its energy.

Dragon's Symbolism: Mystery, Power, and Unity

The Chinese Dragon embodies mystery, vitality, majesty, and wisdom. It thrives on land, in the sea, and in the sky. Dragons symbolise power and unity, reflecting their strength in all aspects of life.

2024 Chinese Zodiac Dragon: Unity and Opportunities

The Year of the Green Dragon signifies unity, cooperation, and shared resources. Collaboration enhances resources and benefits both parties.

Dragon's Interaction with 2024: Challenges and Humility

Two Dragons can signify conflict or mutual benefit. Dragons must exercise humility to navigate challenges. Solid relationships and careful conflict resolution are essential.

General Fortune for the Dragon: Humility and Prosperity

Forge good relationships with humility. Leverage your reputation and credibility to develop partnerships, ensuring long-term wealth and prosperity.

APRIL Flying Star 3, Discord, Conflict, and Caution

April is hit with double discord with monthly Flying Star 3 joining the annual Flying Star 3. As the celestial dance unfolds, Flying Star 3 takes its place in the cosmic ballet, casting a shadow of tumultuous energies that echo with the resonance of discord. The seeds of gossip, arguments, and legal tribulations find fertile ground to sprout within its realm. This is no benign star; it carries a hostile essence, infamous for weaving a tapestry of violence, anger, and constant disagreements. It ushers in a storm of misunderstandings, heated arguments, and even litigation, casting a shadow over relationships between family members, friends, and colleagues.

The health implications that accompany Flying Star 3 are just as ominous. The liver, gall bladder, feet, and arms may become arenas of discomfort, as this star's presence can manifest in physical malaise. Productivity wanes under its influence as the atmosphere becomes charged with the friction of conflicts.

Marital bonds and familial harmony are trapped in the snare of Flying Star 3's energies. The high-tension atmosphere it fosters casts a pall over relationships between spouses, weakening the foundations of stability within families and marriages. The looming threat of trouble with authorities and potential legal entanglements is a stark reminder of the caution that must be exercised during its reign.

In this dance with celestial forces, July becomes a month where defence and caution are paramount. One can employ various remedies to thwart the negativity carried by Flying Star 3. The traditional Chinese cure, a red piece of paper, can be harnessed to ward off its evil influence. The vibrant hues of red and purple can be woven into the surroundings, manifested through decor objects, candles, and bright lights. The magic flaming wheel, akin to a shield against its negativity, can also be invoked. An image of the fiery red phoenix or the vigilant eagle can stand as guardians of space. And for those who seek an extra layer of protection, the steadfast presence of temple lions and the watchful gaze of an evil eye symbol can be enlisted to keep the darkness at bay.

Pertaining to the Luo Shu or Bagua School of Feng Shui, the annual Flying Star 3 sits in the Centre sector for 2024; this sector represents health, physical, emotional, and spiritual well-being.

The **Centre** of your home should be open and transparent. This allows energy to flow freely and connect all areas. If the power is blocked in the Centre, such as with a staircase or bathroom, try to create as much grounded energy as possible with the Earth Element by using square shapes, earthy colours such as yellow and tan, or objects made from Earth, e.g., ceramic tiles.

04 | APRIL 2024

The Wood Dragon Year

1 Monday
Animal: **Wood Goat**
Flying Star: **2**
Good Day: **Horse**
Bad Day: **Ox**
✈️ ❤️ 🏠

2 Tuesday
Animal: **Fire Monkey**
Flying Star: **3**
Good Day: **Snake**
Bad Day: **Tiger**
✈️ ❤️ 🏠 🏰

3 Wednesday
Animal: **Fire Rooster**
Flying Star: **4**
Good Day: **Dragon**
Bad Day: **Rabbit**

4 Thursday
Animal: **Earth Dog**
Flying Star: **5**
Good Day: **Rabbit**
Bad Day: **Dragon**
⚡

5 Friday
Animal: **Earth Pig**
Flying Star: **6**
Good Day: **Tiger**
Bad Day: **Snake**

6 Saturday
Animal: **Metal Rat**
Flying Star: **7**
Good Day: **Ox**
Bad Day: **Horse**

7 Sunday
Animal: **Metal Ox**
Flying Star: **8**
Good Day: **Rat**
Bad Day: **Goat**

2024 Feng Shui and Chinese Astrology Planner

APRIL MONTHLY CHINESE ZODIAC OVERVIEW

Rat This month's energy offers a more favourable outlook, bringing peace and calm. Understanding your goals and intentions for the year ahead is an excellent time. Be more patient as projects may take longer to develop. Family and loved ones may need more attention at this time.

Ox This can be a challenging month if you wish to make significant changes. Thorough research is necessary before embarking on a new career path. Prioritise safety at home, mainly if there are elderly individuals or children in your household.

Tiger Energy takes a positive upswing, leading you to a happier disposition. Be clear about what you want to achieve and make the most of this month. Money prospects look promising. Personal relationships require heightened attention, mainly due to family demands.

Rabbit You will strongly desire to move forward, but be aware of work disruptions. Adopt a patient and resourceful approach to prevent competition and rivalry with colleagues. Establishing common ground with them is vital for maintaining team productivity. Money energy remains reasonable for most of the month.

Dragon The energy of this month has the potential to stir up a range of emotions within you, leading to heightened sensitivity. Nurturing and managing your emotional well-being is essential during this time. Work or business will go through a competitive phase. Stay tuned to evolving market trends to maintain your edge and progress.

Snake This is a positive and supportive month. It would be best to harness its energy to put your plans or projects into motion. Financially, you can anticipate improvements, with the potential for small, unexpected gains. Relationships are likely to be harmonious, contributing to an overall positive atmosphere.

Horse The energy is unstable this month, and you must be ready for sudden changes to emerge. Events will likely evolve unexpectedly, requiring flexibility and acceptance for solutions to surface. If time permits, a short vacation will be beneficial to your well-being.

Goat If you feel uncertain about the future and experiencing insecurity, consider taking a short vacation or retreat. Stepping away from your daily routine can give you a fresh perspective and help you reconnect with your inner self. Use this time to gain clarity and find renewed inspiration to pursue your dreams and goals.

04 | APRIL 2024

The Wood Dragon Year

8 Monday
Animal: **Water Tiger**
Flying Star: **9**
Good Day: **Pig**
Bad Day: **Monkey**
✈️ ❤️ 🏠

9 Tuesday
Animal: **Water Rabbit**
Flying Star: **1**
Good Day: **Dog**
Bad Day: **Rooster**
✈️ ❤️ 🎬

10 Wednesday
Animal: **Wood Dragon**
Flying Star: **2**
Good Day: **Rooster**
Bad Day: **Dog**
✈️

11 Thursday
Animal: **Wood Snake**
Flying Star: **3**
Good Day: **Monkey**
Bad Day: **Pig**
🏠 🎬

12 Friday
Animal: **Fire Horse**
Flying Star: **4**
Good Day: **Goat**
Bad Day: **Rat**
✈️ ❤️

13 Saturday
Animal: **Fire Goat**
Flying Star: **5**
Good Day: **Horse**
Bad Day: **Ox**
⚡

14 Sunday
Animal: **Earth Monkey**
Flying Star: **6**
Good Day: **Snake**
Bad Day: **Tiger**
🎬

2024 Feng Shui and Chinese Astrology Planner

Monkey This month calls for a shift in your mindset. When stress arises, you are reminded to release the urge to struggle against it. By adopting a more balanced and patient approach, you will navigate this period more harmoniously and find greater ease in your personal and professional life.

Rooster If you are looking for avenues to enhance your lifestyle, this month presents promising opportunities. Quick and decisive choices will play a pivotal role in your professional life. While there is potential for gains through investments, it is crucial to exercise vigilance and prudence.

Dog This month's energy may fluctuate and cause anxiety and stress. Work can be more demanding, but if you maintain balance and resilience, the situation will likely improve as the month progresses. Prioritise regular exercise and ensure you get enough rest for your well-being.

Pig Focuses on necessary tasks and completes them. Spending quality time with friends and family is essential. Later in the month, the energy will move quickly; try to make the most of this dynamic time. Look after your well-being, especially if life gets hectic.

04 | APRIL 2024

The Wood Dragon Year

15 Monday
Animal: **Earth Rooster**
Flying Star: **7**
Good Day: **Dragon**
Bad Day: **Rabbit**

16 Tuesday
Animal: **Metal Dog**
Flying Star: **8**
Good Day: **Rabbit**
Bad Day: **Dragon**
⚡

17 Wednesday
Animal: **Metal Pig**
Flying Star: **9**
Good Day: **Tiger**
Bad Day: **Snake**

18 Thursday
Animal: **Water Rat**
Flying Star: **1**
Good Day: **Ox**
Bad Day: **Horse**
🎬

19 Friday
Animal: **Water Ox**
Flying Star: **2**
Good Day: **Rat**
Bad Day: **Goat**

20 Saturday
Animal: **Wood Tiger**
Flying Star: **3**
Good Day: **Pig**
Bad Day: **Monkey**
✈️🏠✂️❤️🎬

21 Sunday
Animal: **Wood Rabbit**
Flying Star: **4**
Good Day: **Dog**
Bad Day: **Rooster**
✂️🎬

FENG SHUI PRINCIPLES FOR THE BEDROOM

The feng shui in your bedroom is of utmost importance, given that it's where you spend your most vulnerable and restorative hours. Tailoring feng shui principles to your style can enhance the overall energy and luck in your bedroom's decor.

Essential General Tips for the Bedroom:

Ensure your bedroom is of regular shape without missing corners for balanced energy flow.

Keep plants and flowers out of the bedroom, as they can drain your energy, leaving you fatigued despite a good night's sleep.

Choose a bed that is the right size for you; one that is too small may hinder personal growth, while an overly large bed can contribute to relationship issues.

Opt for bedroom furniture with rounded edges and corners, avoiding overly angular designs to prevent the formation of harmful poison arrows that may lead to serious illness if left uncorrected.

Position the bed with the headboard against a wall, avoiding a "floating" arrangement in the centre of the bedroom.

Orient your bed to one of your auspicious directions for a more harmonious sleeping experience.

Minimise or avoid mirrors in the bedroom; place them inside a cabinet if necessary. Ensure that mirrors, especially on dressing tables, do not directly face the bed, as exposed mirrors may invite interference in your relationships.

Choose neutral and relaxing colours for the bedroom to maintain a balanced energy. Avoid excessive Yang energy, which disrupts sleep patterns and keeps you awake at night.

04 | APRIL 2024

The Wood Dragon Year

22 Monday
Animal: **Fire Dragon**
Flying Star: **5**
Good Day: **Rooster**
Bad Day: **Dog**
✈️⚡

23 Tuesday
Animal: **Fire Snake**
Flying Star: **6**
Good Day: **Monkey**
Bad Day: **Pig**

24 Wednesday
Animal: **Earth Horse**
Flying Star: **7**
Good Day: **Goat**
Bad Day: **Rat**
✈️❤️

25 Thursday
Animal: **Earth Goat**
Flying Star: **8**
Good Day: **Horse**
Bad Day: **Ox**

26 Friday
Animal: **Metal Monkey**
Flying Star: **9**
Good Day: **Snake**
Bad Day: **Tiger**
🗳️

27 Saturday
Animal: **Metal Rooster**
Flying Star: **1**
Good Day: **Dragon**
Bad Day: **Rabbit**

28 Sunday
Animal: **Water Dog**
Flying Star: **2**
Good Day: **Rabbit**
Bad Day: **Dragon**
⚡

04 | APRIL 2024

The Wood Dragon Year

29 Monday	Animal: **Water Pig** Flying Star: **3** Good Day: **Tiger** Bad Day: **Snake**
30 Tuesday	Animal: **Water Rat** Flying Star: **4** Good Day: **Ox** Bad Day: **Horse** ✈
1 Wednesday	Animal: **Wood Ox** Flying Star: **5** Good Day: **Rat** Bad Day: **Goat** ⚡
2 Thursday	Animal: **Fire Tiger** Flying Star: **6** Good Day: **Pig** Bad Day: **Monkey** ✈ ❤ 🎬
3 Friday	Animal: **Fire Rabbit** Flying Star: **7** Good Day: **Dog** Bad Day: **Rooster** ✈ 🎬
4 Saturday	Animal: **Earth Dragon** Flying Star: **8** Good Day: **Rooster** Bad Day: **Dog**
5 Sunday	Animal: **Earth Snake** Flying Star: **9** Good Day: **Monkey** Bad Day: **Pig**

MAY 6 - JUNE 5 IS MONTH OF THE SNAKE

SNAKE Chinese Horoscope 2024: Growth and Transformation

(1917, 1929, 1941, 1953, 1965, 1977, 1989, 2001, 2013, 2025, 2037)

In the Year of the Wood Dragon 2024, Snakes will experience positive transformation and growth. The Wood element complements the Snake's natural qualities, offering numerous personal and professional opportunities. Flexibility and embracing change are crucial to success this year.

Career and Professional Growth

Snakes can expect career growth and victories in 2024. Leveraging their strengths and natural skills will lead to success. They should embrace new challenges and seize opportunities aligned with their goals and values.

Financial Outlook and Caution

Financially, 2024 presents opportunities for Snakes, but they must exercise caution and avoid unnecessary risks. Savings and investments in stable sectors are recommended. Wise financial management is essential.

Love and Relationships

Challenges may arise in love and relationships. Effective communication, honesty, and loyalty are crucial. Snakes should stay humble and open, overcoming stubborn tendencies for healthy relationships. The year encourages growth in friendships and associations.

Career Advancement and Transformation

The Wood Dragon year brings opportunities and challenges to the Snake's career. Their intelligence and creativity shine, especially in fields requiring attention to detail. Embracing change and pursuing further education will lead to professional growth.

Wealth and Investment Opportunities

Financial upliftment opportunities arise, but caution is advised due to the Dragon's unpredictable nature. Only invest in robust sectors after thorough research. Innovative thinking can lead to unique income sources.

Health and Wellness

The Snake's enthusiastic energy may lead to physical and emotional fatigue. Prioritising self-care and adapting to changes is essential. Regular exercise and outdoor activities contribute to well-being.

Symbolism of the Snake

In 2024, the Snake symbolises selflessness, enthusiasm, and ambition. Its interaction with the Dragon brings partnership and cooperation, benefiting both parties.

For Snakes, 2024 is a year of dynamic growth and opportunities. Navigating challenges with humility and openness will lead to successful outcomes.

MAY Flying Star 2, From Turmoil to Auspicious Energies

May welcome the auspicious energies of the transformative Flying Star 2; in the intricate cosmic choreography of Flying Stars, the enigmatic Star 2 takes centre stage as it undergoes a profound transformation in 2024. With the advent of Period 9, this once inauspicious star dons a new mantle of auspiciousness, heralding a transition that demands nuanced adjustments. Balancing earth and metal influences is delicate as the pendulum swings from adversity to favour. This choreography requires finesse to prevent one element from overpowering the other.

The significance of this transformation is to be considered. Once considered a precursor of turbulence, negative energy, and affliction in Period 8, Star 2 now emerges as an agent of positive change in Period 9. This shift resembles a rebirth, a phoenix-like resurgence that remarkably supports health and well-being, contrasting the adversities it once represented.

In the realm of Period 9, the intrinsic nature of Star 2 retains its Earth element essence, wielding its influence to evoke energies that once wreaked havoc on health and tranquillity. The initial phases of Period 9 are characterised by residual turbulence as this renewed star continues to bring forth challenges, albeit less dire than before.

For the year 2024, the celestial canvas of Star 2 projects its energies primarily onto the eldest son and individuals born under the Rabbit sign. Its sphere of influence extends to spaces like the East-facing front doors, main bedrooms, and living areas, leaving a subtle imprint on the lives of those it touches. The potential for property and honest estate-related endeavours emerges on the horizon, yet health may be the toll paid for such gains.

A symphony of remedies is advised to harness this transformative star's positive potential. A Health Gourd, or Wu Lou, symbolises healing and well-being, accompanied by Six Gold Coins on a vibrant red tassel. A Saltwater Cure and the benevolent presence of Quan Yin further amplify the harmonising vibrations. Adorning oneself with a Wu Lou pendant or amulet is a protective talisman for those born under the Rabbit sign.

Metal elements rise to the forefront as potent countermeasures. The embrace of brass, copper, bronze, or pewter in the form of objects, artworks, and décor items imbues spaces with the essence of stability. Hues of white, silver, and gold harmonise with this transformation, aligning interiors with the new resonance of Star 2 in Period 9.

Pertaining to the Luo Shu or Bagua school of Feng Shui, the annual Flying Star 2 sits in the Southeast sector for 2024; this sector is representative and governed by wealth and prosperity, income, cash flow and earnings.

The **Southeast** belongs to the element of Wood. To tap into money, luck enhances this area with a water picture or water feature; Water strengthens the wood energy, and flowers, plants, green colours, and water tones will also help support the luck. Always make sure the water flow is entering the home and not leaving …

05 | MAY 2024

The Wood Dragon Year

6 Monday
Animal: **Metal Horse**
Flying Star: **1**
Good Day: **Goat**
Bad Day: **Rat**
🧡 ✈️ 🏭

7 Tuesday
Animal: **Metal Goat**
Flying Star: **2**
Good Day: **Horse**
Bad Day: **Ox**

8 Wednesday
Animal: **Water Monkey**
Flying Star: **3**
Good Day: **Snake**
Bad Day: **Tiger**
🏭

9 Thursday
Animal: **Water Rooster**
Flying Star: **4**
Good Day: **Dragon**
Bad Day: **Rabbit**
✈️ 🏠 🧡 / 🏭

10 Friday
Animal: **Wood Dog**
Flying Star: **5**
Good Day: **Rabbit**
Bad Day: **Dragon**
✈️ ⚡ 🏭

11 Saturday
Animal: **Wood Pig**
Flying Star: **6**
Good Day: **Tiger**
Bad Day: **Snake**

12 Sunday
Animal: **Fire Rat**
Flying Star: **7**
Good Day: **Ox**
Bad Day: **Horse**
✈️ 🏠 🧡 🏭

MAY MONTHLY CHINESE ZODIAC OVERVIEW

Rat The energy of this month favours creativity and initiative. Prioritise productivity and accomplish as much as you can. It is also a good time for business networking or to connect with new individuals. At the workplace, you must be nurturing to improve relationships with colleagues.

Ox During this month, you will experience supportive energy that you can harness to empower yourself. Be positive, as you will receive more support from others, bolstering your confidence as you advance with your envisioned projects. The financial outlook is moderate.

Tiger This month may bring uncertainty, potentially leaving you restless. Minor setbacks could arise at work but are likely to be resolved independently. For business owners, embracing fresh ideas and opportunities is crucial. Travel is on the horizon, but exercise caution with your belongings.

Rabbit This month's energy presents greater extremes than the previous one as it can potentially challenge your visions. The key to success is to be confident and focus on your objectives. Maintaining good interpersonal relationships will remain crucial. Expect heightened demands from family or loved ones during this period.

Dragon This high-energy month holds exceptional significance, particularly in finances. While there is potential for gains, there is also indication of problems. Be careful of a possible misleading scenario that could lead to troublesome situations. It is advisable to delve deeper into the details before jumping to conclusions.

Snake In this month, you might experience joyful moments and challenges that will keep you engaged. Taking good care of your physical well-being is essential, as backaches and pains are possible. Work and business affairs might progress slower, but remaining patient and avoiding impulsive decisions is critical.

Horse You are moving into a more supportive phase, and adopting a more optimistic and open mindset would be beneficial. It is an opportune time for job seekers and those seeking career advancement. It is also important to remain cautious and aware of changes in your surroundings so as not to overlook any significant opportunities that might arise.

Goat Overall, this month brings a positive atmosphere for both your professional life and financial outlook. As energy moves quickly, you must balance your professional and personal responsibilities. Family might require more attention, and you must make time for them.

05 | MAY 2024

The Wood Dragon Year

13 Monday
Animal: **Fire Ox**
Flying Star: **8**
Good Day: **Rat**
Bad Day: **Goat**
✈/🎬

14 Tuesday
Animal: **Earth Tiger**
Flying Star: **9**
Good Day: **Pig**
Bad Day: **Monkey**

15 Wednesday
Animal: **Earth Rabbit**
Flying Star: **1**
Good Day: **Dog**
Bad Day: **Rooster**
✈/❤️

16 Thursday
Animal: **Metal Dragon**
Flying Star: **2**
Good Day: **Rooster**
Bad Day: **Dog**
✈🏠❤️🎬

17 Friday
Animal: **Metal Snake**
Flying Star: **3**
Good Day: **Monkey**
Bad Day: **Pig**

18 Saturday
Animal: **Water Horse**
Flying Star: **4**
Good Day: **Goat**
Bad Day: **Rat**
✈/🎬

19 Sunday
Animal: **Water Goat**
Flying Star: **5**
Good Day: **Horse**
Bad Day: **Ox**
⚡

Monkey This month encourages you to approach life with a patient mindset and to make decisions thoughtfully. In your professional life, you must refrain from interfering in the affairs of others. Focusing on personal growth will make you more effective and create a space for positive developments.

Rooster If you are contemplating a shift towards something new, this is the right time to explore. However, it is essential to be discerning when opportunities arise, as not all of them will align with your goals. Mid-month, be aware that a dip in energy may require you to put more effort into projects to get them off the ground.

Dog In this transformative month of fluctuations, be prepared for some changes that may discomfort some individuals. Amidst the shifting energies, it is essential not to let changes impact you physically and mentally. Embrace a self-care routine with sufficient rest, nourishing meals, and regular exercise to replenish and rejuvenate your energy.

Pig At the start of the month, you may feel restless, desiring change. Improving relationships with coworkers is essential. Later in the month, events will move swiftly, so stay focused and meet deadlines. Prioritise personal wellness and take better care of yourself for overall well-being.

05 | MAY 2024

The Wood Dragon Year

20 Monday
Animal: **Wood Monkey**
Flying Star: **6**
Good Day: **Snake**
Bad Day: **Tiger**

21 Tuesday
Animal: **Wood Rooster**
Flying Star: **7**
Good Day: **Dragon**
Bad Day: **Rabbit**

22 Wednesday
Animal: **Wood Dog**
Flying Star: **8**
Good Day: **Rabbit**
Bad Day: **Dragon**

23 Thursday
Animal: **Fire Pig**
Flying Star: **9**
Good Day: **Tiger**
Bad Day: **Snake**

24 Friday
Animal: **Fire Rat**
Flying Star: **1**
Good Day: **Ox**
Bad Day: **Horse**

25 Saturday
Animal: **Earth Ox**
Flying Star: **2**
Good Day: **Rat**
Bad Day: **Goat**

26 Sunday
Animal: **Earth Tiger**
Flying Star: **3**
Good Day: **Pig**
Bad Day: **Monkey**

2024 Feng Shui and Chinese Astrology Planner

05 | MAY 2024

The Wood Dragon Year

27 Monday
Animal: **Metal Rabbit**
Flying Star: **4**
Good Day: **Dog**
Bad Day: **Rooster**
✈ / 🎬

28 Tuesday
Animal: **Metal Dragon**
Flying Star: **5**
Good Day: **Rooster**
Bad Day: **Dog**
/ ⚡ ❤

29 Wednesday
Animal: **Water Snake**
Flying Star: **6**
Good Day: **Monkey**
Bad Day: **Pig**

30 Thursday
Animal: **Water Horse**
Flying Star: **7**
Good Day: **Goat**
Bad Day: **Rat**
✈ 🏠 ❤ 🎬

31 Friday
Animal: **Wood Goat**
Flying Star: **8**
Good Day: **Horse**
Bad Day: **Ox**

1 Saturday
Animal: **Fire Monkey**
Flying Star: **9**
Good Day: **Snake**
Bad Day: **Tiger**
🏠 ✈ / ❤ 🎬

2 Sunday
Animal: **Fire Rooster**
Flying Star: **1**
Good Day: **Dragon**
Bad Day: **Rabbit**
✈ / 🎬

JUNE 6 – JULY 6 IS MONTH OF THE HORSE

HORSE Chinese Horoscope 2024: Seizing Opportunities

(1918, 1930, 1942, 1954, 1966, 1978, 1990, 2002. 2014, 2026, 2038)

The upcoming Year of the Wood Dragon in 2024 holds significant changes and opportunities for the Horse. Renowned for their free-spirited and daring nature, Horses can expect a year of volatility and growth.

Vital Changes and Volatility

With its energy and power, the Year of the Wood Dragon presents opportunities for Horses to succeed and prosper. However, caution is advised to navigate unpredictability. Steady progress is preferable to impulsive decisions.

Personal and Professional Challenges

The Horse's personal and professional life will experience fluctuations. Challenges and conflicts may arise in relationships, demanding clear and genuine communication for deeper connections.

Financial Stability and Triumph

In the realm of finances, positive changes await Horses in 2024. Opportunities for growth and stability open up, emphasising the importance of hard work, honesty, and adherence to values.

Love and Relationships

For single Horses, the year brings potential love connections, urging patience and trust-building. Committed Horses may face disputes, emphasising the need for clear communication and patience to overcome challenges.

Career: Progress and Obstacles

Horses should prepare for a challenging career journey in 2024, facing hurdles and opponents. Vigilance and careful navigation are essential, especially for those starting their careers.

Entrepreneurship and Adaptation

Business-minded Horses might encounter unexpected changes, requiring a proactive and rule-abiding approach. Startup ventures demand careful navigation following regulations for progress.

Wealth: Challenges and Creativity

Financially, unexpected challenges might arise, but Horses' resourcefulness can lead to returns from new projects. Strategic investments are advised, with creativity essential to harness Dragon's vitality.

Health and Lifestyle

Horses should be cautious with their health, especially during physical activities. Lifestyle changes are encouraged, including healthy routines, exercise, and a nutritious diet.

Symbolism of the Horse

In 2024, the Horse's speed and Dragon's power vie for leadership, representing their mutual support and achievements.

The Year of the Wood Dragon holds both promise and unpredictability for Horses. Navigating challenges with patience, clear communication, and adaptability will lead to a year of growth and success.

JUNE Flying Star 1, Triumph, Victory, and Brilliance

June Monthly Flying Star 1 emerges as a brilliant beacon of positive influence in the grand tapestry of celestial energies. Known as the Star of Triumph, this divine luminary casts its benevolent rays upon realms of fame, wealth, intelligence, and success. Its presence signals the infusion of uplifting energies that herald a season of growth and accomplishment.

Guided by the auspicious energies of Flying Star 1, individuals find themselves traversing pathways paved with triumph and victory. Its influence extends across various domains, from attaining success and reputation to elevating one's standing, name, and status. The star's radiance mainly illuminates the realms of career and academic pursuits, such as writing, research, and scholarly endeavours. Within this celestial dance, the resonance of Flying Star 1 fosters an environment ripe for achieving laurels of accomplishment.

The optimistic nature of this star does not merely endow one with fleeting successes; it shapes an environment conducive to lasting triumphs. Be it surmounting competition, realising aspirations, or nurturing wealth opportunities, the dynamic energy of Flying Star 1 cultivates an atmosphere where influence and victory converge. Those who bask in the embrace of this star's points are propelled toward engaging in noble pursuits and endeavours that beckon wealth and career advancements. If you happen to be the eldest son or bear the Rabbit zodiac sign, the resonance of this star aligns with your endeavours, prompting you to embrace competitive activities with zest.

While Flying Star 1 augments the pursuit of victory over health concerns and malaise, navigating potential emotional turbulences with mindfulness is essential. Emotional stability takes centre stage, and vigilance against depression becomes paramount.

The elemental essence of Flying Star 1 is Water; triumph finds its expression through this conduit. Its potential can be activated by channelling Yang's energy into this promising star. The stage for victory is set by introducing metallic elements–windchimes, collections of trophies, or medals. As the waters flow, a water feature or the presence of a Victory Horse figurine accompanied by a Ruyi symbolises the alignment of energies that pave the way for triumph and prosperity.

Pertaining to the Luo Shu or Bagua School of Feng Shui, the annual Flying Star 1 sits in the East sector for 2024; this sector is representative of good health and longevity.

The **East** belongs to Wood, which enhances positive health and well-being by strengthening with water and wood; therefore, bamboo in Water is a powerful cure. Greenery, plants, and flowers are also acceptable to enhance the sector. The east sector is the home of the celestial green dragon, so placing the symbolism of the dragon in the East can maximise the family's luck. A Quan Yin can also be used to safeguard health and well-being.

06 | JUNE 2024

The Wood Dragon Year

3 Monday
Animal: **Earth Dog**
Flying Star: **2**
Good Day: **Rabbit**
Bad Day: **Dragon**
✈🏠⚡❤🏯

4 Tuesday
Animal: **Earth Pig**
Flying Star: **3**
Good Day: **Tiger**
Bad Day: **Snake**

5 Wednesday
Animal: **Metal Rat**
Flying Star: **4**
Good Day: **Ox**
Bad Day: **Horse**

6 Thursday
Animal: **Metal Ox**
Flying Star: **5**
Good Day: **Rat**
Bad Day: **Goat**
⚡❤🏯

7 Friday
Animal: **Water Tiger**
Flying Star: **6**
Good Day: **Pig**
Bad Day: **Monkey**
🏯

8 Saturday
Animal: **Water Rabbit**
Flying Star: **7**
Good Day: **Dog**
Bad Day: **Rooster**

9 Sunday
Animal: **Wood Dragon**
Flying Star: **8**
Good Day: **Rooster**
Bad Day: **Dog**
✈❤🏠

JUNE MONTHLY CHINESE ZODIAC OVERVIEW

Rat Be aware that this month's energy can cause emotional discomfort. It is essential to look after your safety and well-being during this time. As money energy is unstable, you must be cautious when investing; hasty decisions should be avoided. A short vacation will be beneficial.

Ox If you have undergone recent changes, your energy may take longer to recharge. Setting clear intentions can accelerate this process and gain momentum towards your goals. Anticipate the potential for additional income or profits.

Tiger This month holds significant power that will increase your chances of productivity and success. Approach change with confidence as you enter a phase of abundance. Work will be fruitful, and profits and gains are indicated. Partnerships are poised to flourish.

Rabbit The energy of this month prompts you to contemplate your life journey. Are you aligning with your dreams and goals? As the month progresses, you will have the opportunity to revisit events that you have temporarily set aside. Prioritise networking, as expanding your circle of contacts is essential now.

Dragon The energy of this month is calmer and favourable. It is a reasonable period if you plan to push new ideas and products. Plans you previously put on hold can now be revived, but exercise caution and meticulously review all documents before putting your signature on the dotted line. This is an excellent time to formulate practical plans for the rest of the year.

Snake The stable energy of this month will have a more positive outlook. Confidence and embracing flexibility without compromising focus will be vital in navigating any unforeseen twists. Financially, the energy suggests stability, and it is an excellent time to review your financial plans.

Horse It is an excellent time to review your dreams and hopes. If you have been disappointed with an aspect of your life that has not been working for you. be careful of whom you put your trust. Workwise, there are indications that you will be let down this month. You should also beware that events can go through twists and turns before reaching outcomes.

Goat This month holds promising energy for you. Whether mapping out your career path or setting long-term goals, dedicating time to envisioning your future can be highly beneficial. In your professional life, you can expect to experience a positive phase with supportive people around you.

06 | JUNE 2024

The Wood Dragon Year

10 Monday
Animal: **Wood Snake**
Flying Star: **9**
Good Day: **Monkey**
Bad Day: **Pig**
❤️🎬

11 Tuesday
Animal: **Fire Horse**
Flying Star: **1**
Good Day: **Goat**
Bad Day: **Rat**

12 Wednesday
Animal: **Fire Goat**
Flying Star: **2**
Good Day: **Horse**
Bad Day: **Ox**
✈️🏠✂️❤️🎬

13 Thursday
Animal: **Earth Monkey**
Flying Star: **3**
Good Day: **Snake**
Bad Day: **Tiger**
✈️✂️🏠

14 Friday
Animal: **Earth Rooster**
Flying Star: **4**
Good Day: **Dragon**
Bad Day: **Rabbit**

15 Saturday
Animal: **Metal Dog**
Flying Star: **5**
Good Day: **Rabbit**
Bad Day: **Dragon**
✈️🏠✂️⚡❤️🎬

16 Sunday
Animal: **Metal Pig**
Flying Star: **6**
Good Day: **Tiger**
Bad Day: **Snake**
✈️🏠🎬

Monkey Patience and persistence are needed this month, especially when dealing with work or business projects. The financial outlook is unstable, and it is essential to manage your spending wisely. This is also not the best time for partnerships or collaborative ventures.

Rooster You might find it hard to move forward as life is tugging you in two distinct directions. To help yourself, you could use this time to reconnect with your passions, nurture your relationships, and invest time in self-care. Maintaining a positive outlook and staying focused will help you.

Dog At the workplace, adopt a positive outlook to tackle any obstacles that come your way. Lowering your expectations can help manage disappointments and foster a more balanced perspective. New opportunities for meeting new people or forming new relationships are indicated, so stay open to these possibilities. Someone may bring you unexpected good news that can brighten your journey.

Pig Emotionally, you might feel a bit stifled. To pursue a career change, be more proactive and take initiative. Expect tougher competition in business, particularly in retail. Short work-related trips are likely. Stay open to opportunities and be prepared for challenges.

06 | JUNE 2024

The Wood Dragon Year

17 Monday
Animal: **Water Rat**
Flying Star: **7**
Good Day: **Ox**
Bad Day: **Horse**

18 Tuesday
Animal: **Water Ox**
Flying Star: **8**
Good Day: **Rat**
Bad Day: **Goat**

19 Wednesday
Animal: **Wood Tiger**
Flying Star: **9**
Good Day: **Pig**
Bad Day: **Monkey**

20 Thursday
Animal: **Wood Rabbit**
Flying Star: **1**
Good Day: **Dog**
Bad Day: **Rooster**

21 Friday
Animal: **Fire Dragon**
Flying Star: **2/8**
Good Day: **Rooster**
Bad Day: **Dog**

22 Saturday
Animal: **Fire Snake**
Flying Star: **7**
Good Day: **Monkey**
Bad Day: **Pig**

23 Sunday
Animal: **Earth Horse**
Flying Star: **6**
Good Day: **Goat**
Bad Day: **Rat**

06 | JUNE 2024

The Wood Dragon Year

24 Monday
Animal: **Earth Goat**
Flying Star: **5**
Good Day: **Horse**
Bad Day: **Ox**
✈️ ✂️ ⚡ 🏠 ❤️ 🎬

25 Tuesday
Animal: **Metal Monkey**
Flying Star: **4**
Good Day: **Snake**
Bad Day: **Tiger**
✈️ ❤️ 🏠

26 Wednesday
Animal: **Metal Rooster**
Flying Star: **3**
Good Day: **Dragon**
Bad Day: **Rabbit**
❤️

27 Thursday
Animal: **Water Dog**
Flying Star: **2**
Good Day: **Rabbit**
Bad Day: **Dragon**
✈️ ✂️ ⚡ ❤️ 🏠

28 Friday
Animal: **Water Pig**
Flying Star: **1**
Good Day: **Tiger**
Bad Day: **Snake**

29 Saturday
Animal: **Wood Rat**
Flying Star: **9**
Good Day: **Ox**
Bad Day: **Horse**

30 Sunday
Animal: **Wood Ox**
Flying Star: **8**
Good Day: **Rat**
Bad Day: **Goat**
✈️ 🎬

2024 Feng Shui and Chinese Astrology Planner

JULY 7 – AUGUST 7 IS MONTH OF THE GOAT

GOAT Chinese Horoscope 2024: Guided by the Dragon

(1919, 1931, 1943, 1955, 1967, 1979, 1991, 2003, 2015, 2027, 2039)

Goats are characterised by their shyness, kindness, determination, and adaptability. They exhibit endurance and self-motivation and are known for weathering hardships. In Chinese astrology, the Goat is often called the "Wood's Storage Room," containing Yin Earth, Yin Fire, and Yin Wood elements.

Dragon and Goat: A Symbiotic Relationship

The Chinese Dragon, a creature that spans land, sea, and sky, prefers to remain hidden among clouds, representing mystery, vitality, wisdom, and power. The Dragon holds Yang Earth, Yin Water, and Yin Wood elements. Its Earth symbolises towering mountains, while its Yin Water signifies a reservoir.

Symbiotic Balance and Guidance

The Dragon's influence over the Goat is like the rainwater that flows from high mountains to nourish flatlands, representing a mentorship and guidance in the ups and downs of life's journey.

2024 Chinese Zodiac Goat in Dragon Year Prediction

Born in the Year of the Goat, the Green Dragon year of 2024 holds promise and growth for you. Guiding by the Dragon's influence, the humble and diligent Goat can expect rewarding outcomes.

Career and Opportunities

As part of the Earth group, the Goat's career is symbolised by Wood, and the Dragon's Yin Wood and Yin Water elements promise numerous job opportunities. The Dragon is a mentor, aiding career direction and resolving work-related challenges.

Wealth and Prosperity

Earth represents the Goat's wealth, and Yin Water within the Dragon signifies financial gain. The Goat's diligent approach aligned with the Dragon's prosperity can produce rewarding economic outcomes.

Love and Relationships

The Goat's Earth represents females, and Yin Wood within the Dragon indicates potential partners through friends. Active participation in social activities increases the likelihood of meeting compatible individuals.

Social Dynamics and Harmony

Goats' supple and generous personalities foster harmony with those of the Tiger, Rabbit, and Horse. While interactions with Dragons might be average, maintaining balance with others ensures popularity within the group.

Health and Well-being

The Earth element influences both Goats and Dragons. To maintain health, attention should be given to digestion and urinary systems. Spending time in natural surroundings aids well-being.

The Year of the Dragon in 2024 offers the Goat opportunities and growth. Guided by the Dragon's influence, Goats can navigate challenges and succeed through diligent efforts and adaptability.

JULY Flying Star 9, Abundant Prosperity and Beyond

July celebrates. In the celestial tapestry, the luminous radiance of Flying Star 9 gleams resplendently. This star, hailed as the emissary of Current Prosperity, casts its brilliant influence over spheres of completion, fame, jubilation, astute wealth, intelligence, popularity, happiness, and acclaim. Operating as a vibrant and captivating Fire Star, its dynamic essence ignites a cascade of celebrations, fosters festivity, and beckons individuals to gather in its auspicious embrace. Recognised as the "Star of Completion," this celestial presence can bring projects initiated earlier to fruition. Within its domain, financial success and an abundance of fortune flourish harmoniously. It effectively magnifies the means of present and forthcoming ventures, nourishing previously sown seeds and catalysing endeavours to bolster income. Particularly impactful for individuals born under the Goat and Monkey sign, Flying Star 9 illuminates with brilliance.

As the preeminent bearer of current prosperity, Flying Star 9 heralds wealth, catalysing heightened business profits and accentuating investments. It also imparts an elevation in fame and recognition, casting its celestial light on the pursuits of individuals. Flying Star 9 is the epitome of potency among the divine entities in the present configuration. Recommendations abound to frequently engage with spaces influenced by this star, particularly for those embarking on new entrepreneurial ventures, contemplating matrimonial unions, or commencing their journey into parenthood. The augmentation of this star's energy is achieved through the integration of wealth-related symbolism, such as the placement of a wealth jar, the presence of Buddha figurines, a trinity of horses, or 9 Gold Coins arranged on a tassel. Additional enhancers encompass the figure of a Wealth God, Gold Ingots, and objects placed in multiples of nine, all illuminated by vibrant lighting. A symphony of red phoenix symbolism alongside abundant red upholstery and decor amplifies the auspicious vibrations. An exquisite enhancement also lies in incorporating nine fish within a water-based arrangement, lending an unmistakable boost to energy.

Flying Star 9 emerges as a radiant harbinger of prosperity, beckoning individuals to partake in its effervescent energy for a bountiful journey ahead.

Pertaining to the Luo Shu or Bagua school of Feng Shui, the annual Flying Star 9 sits in the Southwest sector for 2024. This sector is representative of relationship luck, love, romance, and marriage.

The **Southwes**t belongs to the element of Earth, to enhance the Southwest of your home for favourable relationship luck. Use earth and fire energy for support: amethyst, rose quartz crystal, or purple, pink, and red peonies. Also, the double happiness symbol, a pair of Mandarin Ducks, symbolises couples. Additional bright lights are recommended in this sector.

07 | JULY 2024

The Wood Dragon Year

1 Monday
Animal: **Fire Tiger**
Flying Star: **7**
Good Day: **Pig**
Bad Day: **Monkey**
✈️💼

2 Tuesday
Animal: **Fire Rabbit**
Flying Star: **6**
Good Day: **Dog**
Bad Day: **Rooster**

3 Wednesday
Animal: **Earth Dragon**
Flying Star: **5**
Good Day: **Rooster**
Bad Day: **Dog**
✈️⚡❤️💼

4 Thursday
Animal: **Earth Snake**
Flying Star: **4**
Good Day: **Monkey**
Bad Day: **Pig**
🏠❤️💼

5 Friday
Animal: **Metal Horse**
Flying Star: **3**
Good Day: **Goat**
Bad Day: **Rat**
✈️

6 Saturday
Animal: **Metal Goat**
Flying Star: **2**
Good Day: **Horse**
Bad Day: **Ox**
✈️❤️🏠

7 Sunday
Animal: **Water Monkey**
Flying Star: **1**
Good Day: **Snake**
Bad Day: **Tiger**
❤️💼

JULY MONTHLY CHINESE ZODIAC OVERVIEW

Rat This month will present you with challenging decisions to make. Despite your inclination, addressing these choices and ensuring they align with your best interests is imperative. Strive to sidestep potential workplace conflicts. Prioritise self-care and nurturing relationships with loved ones during this period.

Ox This month's energy can bring a sense of uncertainty that might lead to indecision. A challenging situation will prompt you to reconsider or abandon an old project or habit. Beware that interpersonal relationships are poised for sensitivity; try to be more understanding and avoid unnecessary conflicts.

Tiger The energy of this period is tranquil. It presents an opportunity to address personal issues. Work or business may experience a slower pace. Devoting quality time to loved ones is paramount. Financially, the positive money energy continues.

Rabbit The energy of this month carries a creative and optimistic tone. Life's events unfold with a sense of ease and comfort. This month is one of your most favourable periods, urging you to maximise its advantages. Business and financial prospects are positive, potentially resulting in increased profits or income.

Dragon The fluctuating energy of this month can affect many born under the Dragon sign. It is essential to maintain a positive outlook even though the power might not align with your preferences. You can navigate this month more effectively by avoiding hasty decisions and conflicts.

Snake The fluctuating energy this month might frustrate you and cause some challenges at work.

Horse At the month's start, you might feel lethargic and lack motivation. As the energy is slow-moving, it is an opportune time to focus on personal tasks and recharge your energy. Relationship stress is indicated this month; therefore, interaction with clients and co-workers must be managed with patience and understanding to prevent misunderstandings.

Goat This month's energy can be sensitive and needs to be managed carefully. Maintaining your energy levels and avoiding dips is essential, as a sudden lack of motivation could hinder your progress. You are also cautioned to avoid engaging in rough or risky sports during this period.

Monkey Some members of the Monkey Sign can struggle with a lack of creativity or enthusiasm during this period. You are encouraged to take time out to recharge your energy. Travel, exercise, and being in the great outdoors will be beneficial.

07 | JULY 2024

The Wood Dragon Year

8 Monday
Animal: **Water Rooster**
Flying Star: **9**
Good Day: **Dragon**
Bad Day: **Rabbit**
✈️ ❤️

9 Tuesday
Animal: **Wood Dog**
Flying Star: **8**
Good Day: **Rabbit**
Bad Day: **Dragon**
⚡ ❤️

10 Wednesday
Animal: **Wood Pig**
Flying Star: **7**
Good Day: **Tiger**
Bad Day: **Snake**
🤸 🏠 🎬

11 Thursday
Animal: **Fire Rat**
Flying Star: **6**
Good Day: **Ox**
Bad Day: **Horse**
🎬

12 Friday
Animal: **Fire Ox**
Flying Star: **5**
Good Day: **Rat**
Bad Day: **Goat**
⚡

13 Saturday
Animal: **Earth Tiger**
Flying Star: **4**
Good Day: **Pig**
Bad Day: **Monkey**
✈️ 🤸 🏠 ❤️ 🎬

14 Sunday
Animal: **Earth Rabbit**
Flying Star: **3**
Good Day: **Dog**
Bad Day: **Rooster**
✈️ 🤸 🏠 ❤️ 🎬

Rooster This month has potential success, but the energy could turn unstable. Be more flexible without compromising your focus; this will be the key to navigating any unforeseen twists. Using this time to strengthen your connections with innovative people would be best.

Dog This month may not be as supportive, and you might be easily irritated. Maintaining a sense of calm within yourself and in your interactions with others is essential. If you are considering a job change, it is best to hold off for now and wait for a more favourable time. A positive mindset will help you navigate challenges and avoid making hasty decisions.

Pig If you seek guidance or direction in decision-making, it is best to let the energy guide you toward potential approaches. Prepare for a hectic phase that may lead to forgetfulness and jot down important dates and tasks. Prioritise your well-being by ensuring adequate rest. Stay organised and mindful to make the most of this month.

07 | JULY 2024

The Wood Dragon Year

15 Monday
Animal: **Metal Dragon**
Flying Star: **2**
Good Day: **Rooster**
Bad Day: **Dog**

16 Tuesday
Animal: **Metal Snake**
Flying Star: **1**
Good Day: **Monkey**
Bad Day: **Pig**

17 Wednesday
Animal: **Water Horse**
Flying Star: **9**
Good Day: **Goat**
Bad Day: **Rat**
🎰

18 Thursday
Animal: **Water Goat**
Flying Star: **8**
Good Day: **Horse**
Bad Day: **Ox**
✈️

19 Friday
Animal: **Wood Monkey**
Flying Star: **7**
Good Day: **Snake**
Bad Day: **Tiger**
✍🏠❤️🎰

20 Saturday
Animal: **Wood Rooster**
Flying Star: **6**
Good Day: **Dragon**
Bad Day: **Rabbit**
❤️

21 Sunday
Animal: **Wood Dog**
Flying Star: **5**
Good Day: **Rabbit**
Bad Day: **Dragon**
⚡

2024 Feng Shui and Chinese Astrology Planner

07 | JULY 2024

The Wood Dragon Year

22 Monday
Animal: **Metal Dragon**
Flying Star: **2**
Good Day: **Rooster**
Bad Day: **Dog**

23 Tuesday
Animal: **Metal Snake**
Flying Star: **1**
Good Day: **Monkey**
Bad Day: **Pig**

24 Wednesday
Animal: **Water Horse**
Flying Star: **9**
Good Day: **Goat**
Bad Day: **Rat**

25 Thursday
Animal: **Water Goat**
Flying Star: **8**
Good Day: **Horse**
Bad Day: **Ox**
✈️

26 Friday
Animal: **Wood Monkey**
Flying Star: **7**
Good Day: **Snake**
Bad Day: **Tiger**

27 Saturday
Animal: **Wood Rooster**
Flying Star: **6**
Good Day: **Dragon**
Bad Day: **Rabbit**
❤️

28 Sunday
Animal: **Wood Dog**
Flying Star: **5**
Good Day: **Rabbit**
Bad Day: **Dragon**
⚡

AUGUST 8 - SEPTEMBER 7 IS MONTH OF THE MONKEY

MONKEY Chinese Horoscope 2024: Dynamic Opportunities and Challenges

(1920, 1932, 1944, 1956, 1968, 1980, 1992, 2004, 2016, 2028, 2040)

The Monkey's Chinese Horoscope for 2024 predicts a year of dynamism and opportunity accompanied by challenges. The Monkey must navigate carefully, relying on strengths and using its natural talents. Challenges in the professional realm can be overcome through diligence, honesty, hard work, and determination.

Career Focus: Building Bonds for Growth

Building solid relationships with colleagues and bosses is crucial for growth and development in the career arena. Facing some financial volatility, Monkeys should practice cautious spending and wise investments after thorough market research and expert guidance.

Love and Relationships: Navigating the Romantic Landscape

The Monkey's love horoscope for 2024 suggests opportunities and challenges. Singles can expect exciting romantic encounters driven by their charm and charisma. Open-mindedness and patience in commitment are vital. Committed relationships are poised for growth through open communication and understanding. Married Monkeys may experience ups and downs, emphasising patience, compromise, and rejuvenating the relationship.

Career Outlook: Navigating Opportunities and Challenges

The Monkey's intelligence, resourcefulness, and adaptability are crucial professionally. 2024 holds potential for growth, advancement, and new ventures. Seizing opportunities, networking, and embracing innovation are essential for career success.

Finance Strategies: Navigating Financial Terrain

Financially, Monkeys must exercise caution in investments, practising wise money management and making informed decisions. Opportunities for income and career growth are present, but a disciplined approach and mindful budgeting are essential. Long-term planning and restraint in expenses are advised.

Health and Well-being: Prioritizing Wellness

For health, Monkeys should maintain balanced lifestyles. Regular exercise, restful sleep, nutritious diets, and stress reduction through activities like meditation are vital. Regular check-ups, vaccinations, and preventive healthcare are crucial for well-being.

Chinese Zodiac Monkey and Dragon: Symbiotic Connection

The Monkey's association with Yang Metal and the Dragon's Earth element form a symbiotic bond. The Dragon protects and educates the Monkey. The Monkey's contribution to the Dragon's prosperity is symbolised through the analogy of rainwater flowing into a reservoir.

In the Year of the Green Dragon, 2024, Monkeys have a year filled with opportunities and challenges across various aspects of life. Through careful navigation, utilisation of natural talents and responsible decision-making, Monkeys can make the most of the year's potential for growth and success.

AUGUST, Flying Star 8, Abundant Prosperity Unveiled

August's steady prosperity was unveiled with the retiring Flying Star 8. Amid the celestial ensemble, the luminous brilliance of Flying Star 8 radiates resplendently. Bestowed with the mantle of the Star of Prosperity, this cosmic entity unveils an encompassing aura of wealth, well-being, luxury, renown, financial prowess, and unwavering prosperity. Its luminosity ushers forth an abundant cascade of affluence, monetary abundance, fortune, and the promising embrace of wealth, nobility, and enduring stability. Under its benevolent influence, anticipations align for the augmentation of income, the attainment of wealth triumphs, and the fortunate alignment of power. As its radiance resonates, professional endeavours burgeon, bolstering reputation and the acknowledgment of diligent efforts. To harness this favourable tide is to unveil a realm of flourishing potential.

For homes that boast a North-facing main door or harbour a living or family area within this sector, the optimistic energy of Flying Star 8 becomes an all-encompassing boon. Particularly promising for individuals who fall under the middle son category or are born under the Rat zodiac sign, this star's blessings extend benevolently.

Preserving this space clutter-free is paramount to ensuring a seamless energy flow. To activate and amplify its auspicious vibrations, the incorporation of diverse wealth-related symbols stands as a potent enhancer. These might encompass a Buddha figurine, a tassel adorned with 6 Gold Coins, a figure of a Wealth God, or Gold Ingots. Additionally, the strategic positioning of bright lights, clocks, and televisions and fostering an environment bustling with activity imparts an unmistakable boost. Notably, the movement remains the most potent conductor of energy, whether through footsteps or other dynamic interactions.

The radiance of Flying Star 8 unveils an arena of luxury and affluence. To embrace its blessings is to enter a realm of enduring prosperity and unyielding success.

Pertaining to the Luo Shu or Bagua School of Feng Shui, the annual Flying Star 8 sits in the North sector for 2024. This sector is representative of career and business luck.

The **North** belongs to the element of Water. To enhance the North of your home for career and business support and luck, place metal colours like white, silver, gold, pewter, bronze and black to support the water energy, or metal decor objects with blue-black tones or water pictures and décor items. A Black Tortoise or Dragon Tortoise piece can also be used.

07 | JULY 2024

The Wood Dragon Year

29 Monday
Animal: **Water Horse**
Flying Star: **6**
Good Day: **Goat**
Bad Day: **Rat**

30 Tuesday
Animal: **Wood Goat**
Flying Star: **5**
Good Day: **Horse**
Bad Day: **Ox**
✈️⚡❤️

31 Wednesday
Animal: **Wood Monkey**
Flying Star: **4**
Good Day: **Snake**
Bad Day: **Tiger**
🎬

1 Thursday
Animal: **Fire Rooster**
Flying Star: **3**
Good Day: **Dragon**
Bad Day: **Rabbit**
✈️✂️❤️

2 Friday
Animal: **Earth Dog**
Flying Star: **2**
Good Day: **Rabbit**
Bad Day: **Dragon**
⚡❤️

3 Saturday
Animal: **Earth Pig**
Flying Star: **1**
Good Day: **Tiger**
Bad Day: **Snake**
✈️✂️🎬

4 Sunday
Animal: **Metal Rat**
Flying Star: **9**
Good Day: **Ox**
Bad Day: **Horse**
🎬

AUGUST MONTHLY CHINESE ZODIAC OVERVIEW

Rat This month offers a relatively smooth journey for you, although workplace dynamics might still be challenging due to differences in opinions. Maintaining a positive and adaptable attitude can earn you respect. If your energy wanes during the execution of specific projects, reconsider the approach.

Ox Your energy might fluctuate occasionally this month. It is essential to keep an optimistic and strong mindset this month. Expect more robust competition, but be confident that the positive energy of this time will carry you through successfully.

Tiger This month's energy might leave you feeling fatigued, so prioritise rest and time away from screens. You may experience a reluctance toward a current project, but you cannot decide if you should abandon it. Financially, energy is low; therefore, refrain from taking risks; there could be extra expenses.

Rabbit This month presents challenges to your visions and goals. Utilise this period for reflection and assess whether you are on the right path to achieve your aspirations. In your professional life, collaboration is encouraged for work to flow smoothly. Financially, the money energy remains stable throughout this period.

Dragon Events will move noticeably faster this month, and you will be called to make swift decisions. Your work commitments will keep you entirely occupied. It is crucial to be self-confident, especially in decision-making. Prioritise your safety and avoid participating in high-impact activities.

Snake The energy this month brings a lighter and more optimistic atmosphere than the previous month. Your financial situation is stable, ensuring a consistent income. With increased activity in store for your zodiac sign, you might find yourself busier than usual. Travel opportunities are indicated. A short getaway to unwind and relax could prove beneficial if circumstances allow.

Horse This month holds promising prospects across various aspects of your life. You will see positive outcomes with an optimistic approach, financial prudence, and a dedicated work ethic. Make sure you embrace the positive energy surrounding you and make the most of the opportunities that come your way.

Goat The energy can fluctuate more drastically this month, and it is advisable to maintain a flexible and adaptable approach. Going with the flow can help you manage the ups and downs of events more effectively. You must be cautious and avoid making impulsive investment decisions, as money energy can be volatile.

08 | AUGUST 2024

The Wood Dragon Year

5 Monday
Animal: **Metal Ox**
Flying Star: **8**
Good Day: **Rat**
Bad Day: **Goat**

6 Tuesday
Animal: **Water Tiger**
Flying Star: **7**
Good Day: **Pig**
Bad Day: **Monkey**

7 Wednesday
Animal: **Water Rabbit**
Flying Star: **6**
Good Day: **Dog**
Bad Day: **Rooster**

8 Thursday
Animal: **Wood Dragon**
Flying Star: **5**
Good Day: **Rooster**
Bad Day: **Dog**

9 Friday
Animal: **Wood Snake**
Flying Star: **4**
Good Day: **Monkey**
Bad Day: **Pig**

10 Saturday
Animal: **Fire Horse**
Flying Star: **3**
Good Day: **Goat**
Bad Day: **Rat**

11 Sunday
Animal: **Fire Goat**
Flying Star: **2**
Good Day: **Horse**
Bad Day: **Ox**

Monkey You are entering a more positive and productive phase, so it is an excellent time to move forward with your plans and initiatives. This is also a perfect time to make new connections, and you should make full use of this time to meet new people and expand your social or business circle.

Rooster The energy of this month is prone to fluctuations, requiring you to have a more positive mindset. Focus your energy towards what you wish to manifest, and consciously release any lingering negative thoughts. Taking good care of your well-being is essential, as this is a draining period.

Dog This month's energy is filled with encouragement, and you will feel more optimistic. Money energy remains relatively low on the financial front, so it is essential to continue being prudent with your expenses and financial decisions. If you are in business and feel tempted to take a chance and consider expanding, it is advisable to hold off for now.

Pig This high-energy month continues your positive phase. Review and set new goals for your immediate future. Expect recognition and accolades. You may receive good news, especially if you are awaiting results. Travel opportunities are on the horizon. Embrace the energy and make the most of the good options.

08 | AUGUST 2024

The Wood Dragon Year

12 Monday
Animal: **Earth Monkey**
Flying Star: **1**
Good Day: **Snake**
Bad Day: **Tiger**
✈ ⌂

13 Tuesday
Animal: **Earth Rooster**
Flying Star: **9**
Good Day: **Dragon**
Bad Day: **Rabbit**

14 Wednesday
Animal: **Metal Dog**
Flying Star: **8**
Good Day: **Rabbit**
Bad Day: **Dragon**
⚡

15 Thursday
Animal: **Metal Pig**
Flying Star: **7**
Good Day: **Tiger**
Bad Day: **Snake**

16 Friday
Animal: **Water Rat**
Flying Star: **6**
Good Day: **Ox**
Bad Day: **Horse**
✈

17 Saturday
Animal: **Water Ox**
Flying Star: **5**
Good Day: **Rat**
Bad Day: **Goat**
⚡

18 Sunday
Animal: **Wood Tiger**
Flying Star: **4**
Good Day: **Pig**
Bad Day: **Monkey**

IDEAL KITCHEN PLACEMENT IN FENG SHUI

In feng shui, the kitchen is often considered an inauspicious area due to potentially harmful energy generated during activities such as cutting vegetables and meat, washing, and accumulating garbage before disposal. Despite this, kitchens play a crucial role, as strategically placing them in less auspicious locations can help mitigate any potential negative influences in those sectors.

It is essential to avoid placing the kitchen in sectors where it might obstruct access to positive energy. When buying a new home or undertaking renovations, it is advisable to position the kitchen in less favourable areas of the home.

IMPORTANT: Kitchens should never be located in the Northwest (NW) sector, as it signifies 'Fire At Heaven's Gate,' which can harm the Patriarch. Adhering to this principle is a fundamental rule in feng shui.

Optimal Kitchen Locations Based on House-Facing Direction:

North:	SW, W, NE
Northeast:	E, SE, S, N
East:	NE, W, SW
Southeast:	W, NE, SW
South:	SW, NE, W
Southwest:	S, N, E, SE
West:	SE, E, N, S
Northwest:	N, S, SW, E

Kitchen placement should align with the house-facing direction. Remember, the one rule that must not be broken is never locating the kitchen in the NW sector.

08 | AUGUST
2024

The Wood Dragon Year

19
Monday

Animal: **Wood Rabbit**
Flying Star: **3**
Good Day: **Dog**
Bad Day: **Rooster**

20
Tuesday

Animal: **Fire Dragon**
Flying Star: **2**
Good Day: **Rooster**
Bad Day: **Dog**
✍🏠❤️🎬

21
Wednesday

Animal: **Fire Snake**
Flying Star: **1**
Good Day: **Monkey**
Bad Day: **Pig**
✍🏠

22
Thursday

Animal: **Fire Horse**
Flying Star: **9**
Good Day: **Goat**
Bad Day: **Rat**
✈️❤️

23
Friday

Animal: **Earth Goat**
Flying Star: **8**
Good Day: **Horse**
Bad Day: **Ox**
🎬

24
Saturday

Animal: **Earth Monkey**
Flying Star: **7**
Good Day: **Snake**
Bad Day: **Tiger**
✈️

25
Sunday

Animal: **Metal Rooster**
Flying Star: **6**
Good Day: **Dragon**
Bad Day: **Rabbit**
🎬

08 | AUGUST 2024

The Wood Dragon Year

26
Monday

Animal: **Metal Dog**
Flying Star: **5**
Good Day: **Rabbit**
Bad Day: **Dragon**
⚡✈🏠

27
Tuesday

Animal: **Water Pig**
Flying Star: **4**
Good Day: **Tiger**
Bad Day: **Snake**

28
Wednesday

Animal: **Water Rat**
Flying Star: **3**
Good Day: **Ox**
Bad Day: **Horse**
✂🏠✈❤🎬

29
Thursday

Animal: **Wood Ox**
Flying Star: **2**
Good Day: **Rat**
Bad Day: **Goat**
🎬

30
Friday

Animal: **Wood Tiger**
Flying Star: **1**
Good Day: **Pig**
Bad Day: **Monkey**

31
Saturday

Animal: **Fire Rabbit**
Flying Star: **9**
Good Day: **Dog**
Bad Day: **Rooster**
✈✂❤🏠

1
Sunday

Animal: **Earth Dragon**
Flying Star: **8**
Good Day: **Rooster**
Bad Day: **Dog**
✈✂🏠🎬

2024 Feng Shui and Chinese Astrology Planner

SEPTEMBER 8 - OCTOBER 7 IS MONTH OF THE ROOSTER

ROOSTER Chinese Horoscope 2024: Challenges and Opportunities

(1921, 1933, 1945, 1957, 1969, 1981, 1993, 2005, 2017, 2029, 2041)

The Rooster, the tenth sign of the Chinese Zodiac, is known for its hardworking, confident, and exuberant personality. In the Year of the Wood Dragon 2024, challenges and opportunities await the Rooster, with sudden changes and potential for personal and professional growth.

Year of the Wood Dragon: Influences and Traits

The Dragon, symbolising power and fortune and the Wood element's prosperity and expansion suggest the Rooster might face unexpected challenges. However, the Rooster's stamina and traits like perseverance, intelligence, and wisdom will drive personal and professional success.

Career Advancements and Challenges

In the professional sphere, 2024 promises opportunities for career growth and recognition. Hard work and dedication will yield glory and new responsibilities. Yet, challenges and changes may arise, demanding adaptability. Networking, collaboration, and cautious financial decisions are essential for success.

Love and Romance: Navigating Mixed Energies

For love, the Rooster's horoscope predicts a year of mixed energies. Singles can expect new romantic prospects, but patience and honesty are essential. Self-love and growth are also emphasised. Commitment will strengthen relationships, although communication is crucial to avoid disputes. Married Roosters should focus on building strong bonds to overcome obstacles.

Career Prospects: Embracing Growth and Advancement

Roosters' career horoscope highlights the potential for advancement in 2024. Displaying skills, embracing challenges, and stepping out of comfort zones will lead to recognition and rewards. Creativity, openness to learning, and a positive mindset will contribute to personal development.

Financial Strategies: Seeking Stability and Growth

Financially, Roosters can enhance their income through skill development, better job opportunities, or entrepreneurial ventures. Cautious spending, avoidance of risky investments, and prudent savings are advised.

Health and Wellness: Prioritising Balance

The Rooster's health horoscope warns of stress and pressure due to work demands. Balancing work, relaxation, proper nutrition, and exercise is essential for overall well-being. Breathing exercises, meditation, and positive environments contribute to maintaining health.

The Rooster in 2024: Significance and Connection

The Rooster's connection with Yin Metal symbolises precious items, and the time between 5 and 7 in the evening signifies nourishment and enjoyment. The harmonious relationship with the Dragon brings bravery, confidence, and ambitions for a comfortable life.

The Year of the Green Dragon brings both challenges and opportunities for Roosters. By leveraging their innate traits and adapting to changes, Roosters can transform challenges into personal and professional advancement chances. Prioritising self-care, communication, and wise decision-making will contribute to a fulfilling year in 2024.

SEPTEMBER Flying Star 7, A Multitude of Discord and Unrest

September has unrest with the arrival of the monthly Flying Star 7. In the cosmic choreography, the inauspicious Flying Star 7 ushers in a cacophony of conflict, disputes, legal entanglements, ailment, mishaps, theft, and the unsettling resonance of gossip. The shadow cast by Flying Star 7 is deeply apprehended due to its latent potential to sow the seeds of rivalry, thievery, trespass, the erosion of wealth, and even the spectre of violence into the fabric of life. In this phase, the exercise of prudence becomes paramount, a cautious dance to sidestep its treacherous undercurrents. Foremost, this star's unsettling energies manifest most prominently in emotional and physical well-being, a caution especially poignant for those who align with the middle daughter category or bear the Horse zodiac sign. In workplaces, the tide of office politics surges, and the swell of rivalries finds resonance. Prudence in trust becomes a watchword as the lurking spectre of deception and schemes looms close. The South, in particular, emanates this turbulence, and thus, vigilance is the guardian of tranquillity.

Unveiling further facets of its venom, Flying Star 7 unfurls the potential for ailments affiliated with the mouth and teeth, laying the groundwork for the conceivable necessity of hospitalisation or surgical interventions for those bearing preexisting health complications. To circumvent its disruptive energy, traditional remedies assume their pivotal role. Among them, the time-honoured prescription of three pieces of Bamboo nestled within a transparent glass vase of water occurs in the Western domain. The symbolic talisman of the Evil Eye, flanked by seven glass elephants, emerges as an effective countermeasure. Alternatively, the positioning of a Blue Rhinoceros alongside a Blue Elephant sets forth a safeguard against this adverse current. As a final strategic measure, incorporating a water feature offers a means to exhaust the metallic energy pervading this space, ensuring the tranquillity and unimpeded vitality of the surrounding environment.

Pertaining to the Luo Shu or Bagua school of Feng Shui, the annual Flying Star 7 sits in the South sector for 2024. This sector is representative of fame, recognition, and reputation.

The **South** belongs to the element of Fire, to enhance the South of your home for recognition. The South sector is the home of the celestial red phoenix. To triumph over the competition with opportunities, use the statue of Phoenix or a horse picture or statue to bring speed and endurance to your endeavours. Generally, bright lights and objects of red (fire) colours are the most promising in the South. Add more wood elements like plants to balance water and fire energy. Galloping Horses or Horse symbolism is the best enhancement.

09 | SEPTEMBER 2024

The Wood Dragon Year

2 Monday
Animal: **Earth Snake**
Flying Star: **7**
Good Day: **Monkey**
Bad Day: **Pig**

3 Tuesday
Animal: **Metal Horse**
Flying Star: **6**
Good Day: **Goat**
Bad Day: **Rat**

4 Wednesday
Animal: **Metal Goat**
Flying Star: **5**
Good Day: **Horse**
Bad Day: **Ox**

5 Thursday
Animal: **Water Monkey**
Flying Star: **4**
Good Day: **Snake**
Bad Day: **Tiger**

6 Friday
Animal: **Water Rooster**
Flying Star: **3**
Good Day: **Dragon**
Bad Day: **Rabbit**

7 Saturday
Animal: **Wood Dog**
Flying Star: **2**
Good Day: **Rabbit**
Bad Day: **Dragon**

8 Sunday
Animal: **Wood Pig**
Flying Star: **1**
Good Day: **Tiger**
Bad Day: **Snake**

SEPTEMBER MONTHLY CHINESE ZODIAC OVERVIEW

Rat Energy is on the upswing, leading you to a more favourable period. Be ready for a busy and demanding time. For your safety, do not be hasty this month. You may also need to devote additional effort to enhance your connection with friends by dedicating quality time with them.

Ox A remarkable month is unfolding that promises personal success. Long-awaited plans will finally regain traction. You can expect support from others, empowering you to move forward confidently. Patience and understanding will tip events in your favour and bring you the rewards you deserve.

Tiger This month's energy can disrupt various aspects of your life. This energy will compel you to reflect on your aspirations for the upcoming years. It will be beneficial to steer clear of noisy and crowded environments.

Rabbit This period requires a quiet yet attentive approach to facilitate your transformation. Seeking ways to enhance your sense of security is essential during this time. Maintain an optimistic outlook and stay focused on your goals. Partnerships and joint projects are likely to yield positive outcomes.

Dragon Emotionally, you will feel happier this month. It is an ideal time to take time to recharge your energy. Stay away from large groups as conflicts are indicated. Engaging in exercises and outdoor activities can effectively alleviate stress. As the money outlook is average, it will be wise to avoid financial risks.

Snake This is another optimistic month that will lift your spirits in various aspects of life. Those pursuing education will excel in their studies. Those wishing for career development must set clear and positive intentions in envisioning your goals. Flexibility in your approach can further enhance your chances of success.

Horse This month continues to be one of the more favourable periods for you. You will see the rewards you desire if you consciously try to maintain an optimistic outlook. While finances are stable, exercising prudence is still essential. Your social life is expected to be active, with opportunities to make new connections.

Goat This month's energy supports creativity and communication. Remember that your approach to challenges can significantly influence the outcomes you experience. Embracing creativity, open communication, and a lighthearted approach will lead to a more prosperous and fulfilling month.

09 | SEPTEMBER 2024

The Wood Dragon Year

9 Monday
Animal: **Fire Rat**
Flying Star: **9**
Good Day: **Ox**
Bad Day: **Horse**

10 Tuesday
Animal: **Fire Ox**
Flying Star: **8**
Good Day: **Rat**
Bad Day: **Goat**

11 Wednesday
Animal: **Earth Tiger**
Flying Star: **7**
Good Day: **Pig**
Bad Day: **Monkey**

12 Thursday
Animal: **Earth Rabbit**
Flying Star: **6**
Good Day: **Dog**
Bad Day: **Rooster**

13 Friday
Animal: **Metal Dragon**
Flying Star: **5**
Good Day: **Rooster**
Bad Day: **Dog**

14 Saturday
Animal: **Metal Snake**
Flying Star: **4**
Good Day: **Monkey**
Bad Day: **Pig**

15 Sunday
Animal: **Water Horse**
Flying Star: **3**
Good Day: **Goat**
Bad Day: **Rat**

Monkey This month's energy is focused on your healing and growth. If you encounter obstacles or challenges, it is time to slow down and carefully assess whether you need to change your approach. Be open to reflecting on your actions and decisions to ensure they align with your overall well-being and goals.

Rooster The Rooster's energy is vital this month; you must be more patient and adaptable, especially at work. Later this month, you will see that your efforts will begin to yield positive results. You are reminded to look after your well-being to run this month successfully.

Dog This month brings new positive energy, and your overall vitality will be enhanced. Embrace the abundance of energy around you, as it can propel you towards achieving your goals and aspirations. Harmony prevails in your relationships with loved ones and family. Enjoy the moments of togetherness and cherish the bonds you share with those closest to you.

Pig Be extra cautious, especially with risky decisions this month, and refrain from making significant financial commitments, except for buying and selling properties. Be decisive in your professional life, as situations may require precise answers. Avoid conflicts and power struggles; opting for a prudent and harmonious approach will help you navigate this period successfully.

09 | SEPTEMBER 2024

The Wood Dragon Year

16 Monday
Animal: **Water Goat**
Flying Star: **2**
Good Day: **Horse**
Bad Day: **Ox**

17 Tuesday
Animal: **Wood Monkey**
Flying Star: **1**
Good Day: **Snake**
Bad Day: **Tiger**
✈️ 🏠 ❤️ 🎬

18 Wednesday
Animal: **Wood Rooster**
Flying Star: **9**
Good Day: **Dragon**
Bad Day: **Dog**
✈️

19 Thursday
Animal: **Fire Dog**
Flying Star: **8**
Good Day: **Rabbit**
Bad Day: **Dragon**
✈️ ❤️ ⚡ 🎬

20 Friday
Animal: **Fire Pig**
Flying Star: **7**
Good Day: **Tiger**
Bad Day: **Snake**
✏️ ✈️ 🏠

21 Saturday
Animal: **Earth Rat**
Flying Star: **6**
Good Day: **Ox**
Bad Day: **Horse**

22 Sunday
Animal: **Earth Ox**
Flying Star: **5**
Good Day: **Rat**
Bad Day: **Goat**
✈️ 🏠 ✏️ ⚡ ❤️ 🎬

ACTIVATING PEACH BLOSSOM LUCK FOR RELATIONSHIP & MARRIAGE LUCK

Individuals seeking to attract potential life partners for marriage can amplify their Peach Blossom Luck by incorporating their Peach Blossom Animal. This feng shui placement method is also an effective way to encourage your partner to step towards marriage!

Optimal Peach Blossom Enhancers are those embellished with symbols of love and marital joy. For instance, if you fall under the zodiac signs of Ox, Snake, or Rooster, consider placing a Peach Blossom Horse in the South. If your zodiac is Rat, Dragon, or Monkey, featuring a Peach Blossom Rooster in the West is advised.

09 | SEPTEMBER 2024

The Wood Dragon Year

23 Monday	Animal: **Metal Tiger** Flying Star: **4** Good Day: **Pig** Bad Day: **Monkey**
24 Tuesday	Animal: **Metal Rabbit** Flying Star: **3** Good Day: **Dog** Bad Day: **Rooster**
25 Wednesday	Animal: **Water Dragon** Flying Star: **2** Good Day: **Rooster** Bad Day: **Dog** ✈️🏠❤️💼
26 Thursday	Animal: **Water Snake** Flying Star: **1** Good Day: **Monkey** Bad Day: **Pig** ✂️💼
27 Friday	Animal: **Wood Horse** Flying Star: **9** Good Day: **Goat** Bad Day: **Rat** ❤️
28 Saturday	Animal: **Wood Goat** Flying Star: **8** Good Day: **Horse** Bad Day: **Ox**
29 Sunday	Animal: **Fire Monkey** Flying Star: **7** Good Day: **Snake** Bad Day: **Tiger** ❤️

09 | SEPTEMBER 2024

The Wood Dragon Year

30 Monday
Animal: **Fire Rooster**
Flying Star: **6**
Good Day: **Dragon**
Bad Day: **Dog**
✈️

1 Tuesday
Animal: **Earth Dog**
Flying Star: **5**
Good Day: **Rabbit**
Bad Day: **Dragon**
✈️⚡❤️💼

2 Wednesday
Animal: **Earth Pig**
Flying Star: **4**
Good Day: **Tiger**
Bad Day: **Snake**
✂️🏠

3 Thursday
Animal: **Metal Rat**
Flying Star: **3**
Good Day: **Ox**
Bad Day: **Horse**

4 Friday
Animal: **Metal Ox**
Flying Star: **2**
Good Day: **Rat**
Bad Day: **Goat**
💼

5 Saturday
Animal: **Water Tiger**
Flying Star: **1**
Good Day: **Pig**
Bad Day: **Monkey**
💼

6 Sunday
Animal: **Water Rabbit**
Flying Star: **9**
Good Day: **Dog**
Bad Day: **Dragon**

OCTOBER 8 - NOVEMBER 6 IS MONTH OF THE DOG

DOG Chinese Horoscope 2024: Gains and Transformations

(1922, 1934, 1946, 1958, 1970, 1982, 1994, 2006, 2018, 2030, 2042)

The Year of the Wood Dragon 2024 brings significant gains in the professional life of the Dog. Confidence, honesty, and calculated risks are crucial to success. Focus on savings and market knowledge, seeking expert guidance for profitable investments.

Well-being and Recognition

In 2024, Dogs experience success and recognition. Colleagues and superiors admire your efforts, encouraging growth. Stay cheerful, diligent, and goal-focused to overcome obstacles.

Dog and Dragon Dynamics

The Dog symbolises dedication, while the Dragon signifies strength and risk. Challenges and growth opportunities await. The Dragon's vitality motivates Dogs to achieve self-growth and skills development.

Embracing Bravery and Resilience

The Year of the Wood Dragon empowers Dogs to become bolder and resolute. Wisely using the Dragon's strength, Dogs can tap into hidden potential and embrace self-growth and intuition.

Love and Transformations

In love, 2024 offers transformative possibilities. Singles may find unexpected connections, urging them to leave their comfort zones. Relationships grow more profound for those in partnerships. Communication and patience are vital for harmony.

Career Changes and Advancements

Career-wise, Dogs should be open to new job prospects or promotions. Networking and trusted advice play a role. The year presents challenges and opportunities for growth and advancement.

Financial Planning and Growth

Financially, the year requires careful planning. Budgeting, wise investments, and seeking expert advice are crucial. Savings are vital, while diligence and patience lead to favourable financial outcomes.

Prioritising Health and Balance

Maintaining well-being is essential for Dogs. Stress management, regular exercise, and nutritious diets support vitality. Focus on mental and emotional health, seeking relaxation through meditation and yoga.

Harmonising Social Connections

Socially, Dogs flourish, garnering support and friendship. Conflicts are unlikely, but if encountered, prioritise resolution for harmony. The year encourages building a broader network.

The Dog's encounter with the Green Dragon promises a year of challenges and opportunities. With prudent decisions, openness to change, and focus on growth, Dogs can navigate the year successfully.

OCTOBER Flying Star 6, A Radiant Beacon of Authority and Fortune

October welcomes the Flying Star 6, stepping into the spotlight as the month's energy. Flying Star 6 is a celestial entity that ushers in a tide of authority, potency, wealth, and the propitious winds of heaven-borne luck. This luminary phenomenon is poised to be the harbinger of prosperous times, orchestrating a grand symphony of career opportunities and the actualisation of long-held aspirations. In its glorious wake, one can anticipate the infusion of enhanced power, elevated stature, and the shimmering aura of a commendable reputation. As an emissary of prosperity, this star graces the scene with divine favour, endowing its beneficiaries with career luck bestowed straight from the heavens. If your gaze falls upon the youngest-born son or the Ox and Tiger in the zodiac realm, know they are poised to reap its bounteous rewards as this star favours their path.

The veneration of this star's positive attributes can lead to the establishment of a commanding presence, indicative of elevated status and influential sway within social circles. The quintessence of authority is encapsulated within its energetic current.

To breathe life into the latent potential of Flying Star 6, one must infuse it with the vigour of Yang energy, invoking the cadence of life through the harmonious interplay of water features, resonant sounds, and vibrant activities. The traditional enhancers echo through time—be it the dignified visage of a Horse figurine, the subtle allure of Six Gold Coins suspended from a tassel, or the enduring emblem of Gold Ingots.

Yet, with all its radiance, it is imperative to tread with caution. Negative external influences can unexpectedly cast a shadow over Flying Star 6, transforming its blessings into turbulent turns. Such unsettling disruptions can manifest as sudden upheavals or abrupt changes, while the spectre of medical complications, particularly about the kidneys or legs, assumes a foreboding presence.

Pertaining to the Luo Shu or Bagua School of Feng Shui, the annual Flying Star 6 sits in the North-East sector for 2024; this sector represents knowledge, scholarly, learning and education.

As the Northeast belongs to the element of Earth, this location becomes promising. To support and enhance, use a picture of Mountains, a Crystal Globe, a world map, the Chinese saint Luohan or Dragon Carp. Take note if a large tree or missing space blocks the Northeast sector, as you will need help tapping into learning and knowledge.

10 | OCTOBER 2024

The Wood Dragon Year

7 Monday
Animal: **Wood Dragon**
Flying Star: **8**
Good Day: **Rooster**
Bad Day: **Dog**
✈︎ 🏠 ❤️ 🎬

8 Tuesday
Animal: **Wood Snake**
Flying Star: **7**
Good Day: **Monkey**
Bad Day: **Pig**

9 Wednesday
Animal: **Fire Horse**
Flying Star: **6**
Good Day: **Goat**
Bad Day: **Rat**
✈︎ 🏠 ❤️ 🎬

10 Thursday
Animal: **Fire Goat**
Flying Star: **5**
Good Day: **Horse**
Bad Day: **Ox**
⚡

11 Friday
Animal: **Earth Monkey**
Flying Star: **4**
Good Day: **Snake**
Bad Day: **Tiger**
✈︎ 🎬

12 Saturday
Animal: **Earth Rooster**
Flying Star: **3**
Good Day: **Dragon**
Bad Day: **Rabbit**

13 Sunday
Animal: **Metal Dog**
Flying Star: **2**
Good Day: **Rabbit**
Bad Day: **Dragon**
✈︎ ⚡ ❤️ 🏠

OCTOBER MONTHLY CHINESE ZODIAC OVERVIEW

Rat Energy fluctuations are indicated and can slow things down or put obstacles in your path. Specific work projects require additional time to progress. If you are considering new initiatives, doing more research for now is better. A short vacation will be beneficial. Money energy is fair.

Ox This month will see heightened energy fluctuations that may lead to unforeseen events and outcomes. Maintaining a low profile and refraining from risk-taking is critical. Prioritise personal safety by reducing solitary night travel, and pay attention to your diet. Prioritising self-care is crucial during this period.

Tiger Restlessness and irritability might characterise your feelings, yet this phase offers an excellent opportunity for personal growth. Financially, the money energy is reasonable. Work may be stressful during this period. Engaging in moderate sports activities can enhance personal safety.

Rabbit This month revolves around the concept of timing. In business, swift actions and early decisions are crucial to keep up with demands. Be aware that a situation might lead you to believe you have been betrayed. Before concluding, it is advisable to delve deeper into the matter and gain a comprehensive understanding.

Dragon This month is a clashing period for your zodiac sign, which might lead to discomfort for many Dragons. During any clashing months, it is essential to prioritise your well-being and safety. Work could become more stressful, and you might feel impatient, but avoiding confrontations is advisable.

Snake This month's energy brings a sense of unpredictability. Flexibility is the key to navigating this month successfully. Be aware that some events may not unfold as expected. Be cautious when taking on new projects and signing contracts. It is an excellent time to review personal goals and visions.

Horse This month presents a blend of mixed energies that can cause dissatisfaction. It will be wise to moderate your expectations throughout this month. You are also cautioned to be more mindful in decision-making or managing changes at the workplace. You can help yourself by staying focused on your goals and maintaining a positive outlook.

Goat It is essential to prioritise your well-being this month, especially your physical and emotional health. While small work challenges are indicated, you are reminded that maintaining a positive attitude can help to dissolve the obstacles and changes that come your way.

10 | OCTOBER 2024

The Wood Dragon Year

14 Monday
Animal: **Metal Pig**
Flying Star: **1**
Good Day: **Tiger**
Bad Day: **Snake**
✈️🏠

15 Tuesday
Animal: **Water Rat**
Flying Star: **9**
Good Day: **Ox**
Bad Day: **Horse**
✏️

16 Wednesday
Animal: **Water Ox**
Flying Star: **8**
Good Day: **Rat**
Bad Day: **Goat**

17 Thursday
Animal: **Wood Tiger**
Flying Star: **7**
Good Day: **Pig**
Bad Day: **Monkey**
🏰

18 Friday
Animal: **Wood Rabbit**
Flying Star: **6**
Good Day: **Dog**
Bad Day: **Dragon**
🏰

19 Saturday
Animal: **Fire Dragon**
Flying Star: **5**
Good Day: **Rooster**
Bad Day: **Dog**
⚡

20 Sunday
Animal: **Fire Snake**
Flying Star: **4**
Good Day: **Monkey**
Bad Day: **Pig**
🧡

Monkey The current energy might be more temperamental, impacting your mental and emotional well-being. It is essential to be aware of these fluctuations and take steps to manage your emotions. Engaging in uplifting activities and practising mindfulness can help you navigate this period more smoothly.

Rooster This is a calm and promising month with positive outcomes in different aspects of your life. Work or business continues to take up your time and energy. As the last few months have been busy, setting time aside for rest is advisable.

Dog This month's energy clashes with the annual ruling zodiac, which can be turbulent. Some of you will be more affected by the conflict than others. For your safety, avoid trips that are overly adventurous or risky sports. The workplace can be chaotic. A good money deal or venture is indicated.

Pig Life is moving steadily, allowing you to embrace the present moment with a sense of ease and balance. You are reminded to prioritise self-care and well-being, as it will boost your energy and enhance your ability to make sound decisions and navigate any complexities that may arise.

10 | OCTOBER 2024

The Wood Dragon Year

21 Monday
Animal: **Fire Horse**
Flying Star: **3**
Good Day: **Goat**
Bad Day: **Rat**
✈️ ❤️ 🏠

22 Tuesday
Animal: **Earth Goat**
Flying Star: **2**
Good Day: **Horse**
Bad Day: **Ox**
❤️

23 Wednesday
Animal: **Earth Monkey**
Flying Star: **1**
Good Day: **Snake**
Bad Day: **Tiger**
✂️ 🏠 ✈️ ❤️ 🏢

24 Thursday
Animal: **Metal Rooster**
Flying Star: **9**
Good Day: **Dragon**
Bad Day: **Rabbit**
❤️ 🏢

25 Friday
Animal: **Metal Dog**
Flying Star: **8**
Good Day: **Rabbit**
Bad Day: **Dragon**
✈️ ⚡ 🏠

26 Saturday
Animal: **Water Pig**
Flying Star: **7**
Good Day: **Tiger**
Bad Day: **Snake**
✈️

27 Sunday
Animal: **Water Rat**
Flying Star: **6**
Good Day: **Ox**
Bad Day: **Horse**

10 | OCTOBER 2024

The Wood Dragon Year

28 Monday
Animal: **Wood Ox**
Flying Star: **5**
Good Day: **Rat**
Bad Day: **Goat**
⚡

29 Tuesday
Animal: **Wood Tiger**
Flying Star: **4**
Good Day: **Pig**
Bad Day: **Monkey**
🎬

30 Wednesday
Animal: **Fire Rabbit**
Flying Star: **3**
Good Day: **Dog**
Bad Day: **Dragon**
✈️ ❤️ 🎬

31 Thursday
Animal: **Fire Dragon**
Flying Star: **2**
Good Day: **Rooster**
Bad Day: **Dog**

1 Friday
Animal: **Earth Snake**
Flying Star: **1**
Good Day: **Monkey**
Bad Day: **Pig**

2 Saturday
Animal: **Metal Horse**
Flying Star: **9**
Good Day: **Goat**
Bad Day: **Rat**
✈️✂️🏠❤️🎬

3 Sunday
Animal: **Metal Goat**
Flying Star: **8**
Good Day: **Horse**
Bad Day: **Ox**
🏠

2024 Feng Shui and Chinese Astrology Planner

NOVEMBER 7 – DECEMBER 6 IS MONTH OF THE PIG

PIG Chinese Horoscope 2024: Navigating Change and Balance

In the Year of the Wood Dragon 2024, Pigs encounter shifts in career and finance. Embrace these changes for growth. Stay focused, seek guidance, manage finances wisely, and avoid impulsive spending.

Love and Relationships: Harmony and Caution

Love holds both highs and lows. Existing relationships require effort, while new ones have potential. Communication and self-care are key. Exercise caution and choose partners wisely.

Career Prospects: Growth and Recognition

A promising career outlook awaits Pigs in 2024. Showcase skills, learn, and adapt. Upskilling and networking lead to advancement. Hard work receives recognition, and bold moves in business yield success.

Financial Growth and Prudent Choices

Finances flourish, but thorough research is vital. Seek advice for wise investments. Long-term strategies are favoured, while impulsive spending is to be avoided. Budgeting and savings ensure stability.

Health and Wellness: Balanced Approach

Health is promising. Balanced diets, exercise, and stress management are essential. Outdoor activities enhance mental and physical well-being. Avoid overexertion and prioritise self-care.

Feng-Shui Remedies for Prosperity

Incorporate Feng-Shui remedies like water elements and plants for luck and growth. Nurture connections, foster positivity, and enhance prosperity in homes and workspaces.

Embrace Opportunities

The Pig's encounter with the Dragon presents opportunities and growth: balance career, relationships, and well-being. Adapt, seek guidance, and prudently approach decisions for a successful year.

EIGHT ASPIRATIONS FORMULA: UNLOCKING 8 TYPES OF FAVORABLE FORTUNE

Within the Pa Kua's distinct sectors lie specific types of luck. Activate these sectors by showcasing appropriate symbols of good fortune to invite eight distinct forms of auspicious luck into your life.

NOVEMBER Flying Star 5, A Star of Dark Omens and Harbingers of Misfortune

November finds the energy of the Flying Star 5 once again taking centre stage, entering into the intricate tapestry of cosmic powers. The ominous presence of Flying Star 5, commonly recognised as the difficult 5 Yellow Star, casts its malevolent shadow. This harbinger of danger, misfortune, and an array of disorders stands as one of the most treacherous and aggressive celestial phenomena within the realm of Feng Shui. Its reputation precedes it—a harbinger of woes, a herald of bad luck, an orchestrator of obstacles, a weaver of calamities, and a conductor of misadventures.

As its ominous energy unfurls, it weaves a web of adversity and hindrances, casting its baleful influence overall in its wake. This maleficent star exudes a toxic aura that magnetises unfavourable outcomes, particularly inauspicious for the youngest daughter and those born under the Rooster sign. Its pernicious effects are vast and disheartening—ranging from financial loss, business disruption, and betrayals to more dire manifestations like tragic accidents, grave injuries, and even fatal calamities.

A lurking sense of trepidation surrounds the Flying Star 5, as it embodies an array of negative energies that can envelop one's endeavours in a shroud of despair. It is the embodiment of bankruptcy, disloyalty, betrayals, and other harbingers of doom that threaten to overturn even the most stable foundations.

To shield against its ominous grasp, the ancient wisdom of Feng Shui imparts sage advice. Breaking ground or embarking on new renovation projects during the presence of this star is ill-advised, as it may unleash its potent negativity. The most powerful method of managing its influence lies in non-interference—let it lie dormant and undisturbed as much as possible. However, for situations where avoidance isn't feasible, one may seek solace in remedies like the Brass Pagoda, the sombre notes of the Bonze bell, the harmonious melody of metal wind chimes, and the purifying Saltwater Cure. The benevolent presence of Ganesha, the remover of obstacles, can also be invoked to mitigate its dire effects.

To counteract the grip of this adversarial star, heavy metal objects crafted from brass, copper, bronze, or pewter can be strategically placed at the heart of one's abode—the Centre. Radiating metallic artwork, hues, and home décor items can echo the sentiment of resistance against its influences, while measures to minimise Fire and Earth energies diminish its potency.

Pertaining to the Luo Shu or Bagua school of Feng Shui, the annual Flying Star 5 sits in the West sector for 2024; this sector is representative of descendants, family and children luck, and the protection of your current assets and wealth.

The Western sector is the home of the celestial white Tiger, so placing the symbolism of the Tiger in the West can protect the family's luck. Place any wealth symbolism in the western area to assist protection and for the family to remain healthy and strong together. The West belongs to the element of Metal. For 2024, enhance wealth luck with Gold Coins, Gold Ingots, a Wealth God, metallic artwork, paintings or colours. The West wall is a favourable position for family photos in metallic frames.

11 | NOVEMBER 2024

The Wood Dragon Year

4 Monday
Animal: **Water Monkey**
Flying Star: **7**
Good Day: **Snake**
Bad Day: **Tiger**
✈️ ❤️ 🎬

5 Tuesday
Animal: **Water Rooster**
Flying Star: **6**
Good Day: **Dragon**
Bad Day: **Rabbit**
🏠 ❤️ 🎬

6 Wednesday
Animal: **Wood Dog**
Flying Star: **5**
Good Day: **Rabbit**
Bad Day: **Dragon**
✈️ ⚡

7 Thursday
Animal: **Wood Pig**
Flying Star: **4**
Good Day: **Tiger**
Bad Day: **Snake**
✈️

8 Friday
Animal: **Fire Rat**
Flying Star: **3**
Good Day: **Ox**
Bad Day: **Horse**
🏠 ❤️ 🎬

9 Saturday
Animal: **Fire Ox**
Flying Star: **2**
Good Day: **Rat**
Bad Day: **Goat**

10 Sunday
Animal: **Earth Tiger**
Flying Star: **1**
Good Day: **Pig**
Bad Day: **Monkey**
✈️ / 🏠

NOVEMBER MONTHLY CHINESE ZODIAC OVERVIEW

Rat This month brings optimistic and creative energy. Co-workers may need attention. It is essential to offer them your support and appreciation. Financial power is moderate and requires careful management. Your overall luck is favourable, and with determination, you should see positive outcomes.

Ox As the start of the month, you might experience a sudden dip in energy. It is necessary to remain focused and complete tasks that are at hand. Outdoor activities are beneficial to your well-being. Later this month, the power will shift towards a more favourable direction with prospects of new opportunities.

Tiger Exercise heightened caution during negotiations this month as the energy is unsupportive. In business, keeping to your current ventures will prove wiser than embarking on new ones. Trust your inner guidance when making decisions, as external influences might mislead you.

Rabbit Be aware that during this month, you might be prone to emotional upsets. To help yourself, engaging in activities you are passionate about and spending time with close friends can give you more support. Prioritise your well-being. Rash money decisions should be avoided.

Dragon This is a high-energy month and is bound to be eventful, which might feel demanding for many individuals born under the Dragon sign. If you find yourself experiencing high levels of stress, consider taking a short vacation or having a few quiet days to aid in restoring your balance.

Snake The energy this month takes a downturn that could lead to events unfolding at a slower pace. Focus on accomplishing tasks during the day and have adequate rest. Drivers must be extra vigilant on the roads. Avoiding financial risks and maintaining a cautious approach to your money is advisable.

Horse While the energy might experience a slight dip, you can still anticipate a relatively decent month ahead. Expect a fast-paced environment at work where events unfold rapidly, keeping you engaged and busy. However, it is advisable to exercise mindfulness, as indications of misunderstandings are present. Clear communication and attentive listening can help prevent any unnecessary complications.

Goat This is a fast-moving month, and it will propel you forward faster in your professional life and social interactions. This is a favourable time to review your goals, consider your aspirations, and see progress. Setting new standards can motivate you to step out of your comfort zone and actively seek new opportunities.

11

| NOVEMBER |
| 2024 |

The Wood Dragon Year

11
Monday

Animal: **Earth Rabbit**
Flying Star: **9**
Good Day: **Dog**
Bad Day: **Rooster**
✈ 🏠 ❤️ 💼

12
Tuesday

Animal: **Metal Dragon**
Flying Star: **8**
Good Day: **Rooster**
Bad Day: **Dog**

13
Wednesday

Animal: **Metal Snake**
Flying Star: **7**
Good Day: **Monkey**
Bad Day: **Pig**

14
Thursday

Animal: **Water Horse**
Flying Star: **6**
Good Day: **Goat**
Bad Day: **Rat**
✈ 🏠 ❤️ 💼

15
Friday

Animal: **Water Goat**
Flying Star: **5**
Good Day: **Horse**
Bad Day: **Ox**
⚡

16
Saturday

Animal: **Wood Monkey**
Flying Star: **4**
Good Day: **Snake**
Bad Day: **Tiger**

17
Sunday

Animal: **Wood Rooster**
Flying Star: **3**
Good Day: **Dragon**
Bad Day: **Rabbit**

Monkey This month is likely to be busy, and the energy appears to move in unpredictable patterns. It is essential to maintain your momentum until the energy shifts, and things will start to fall into place quickly. Meanwhile, stay optimistic in your work environment and be receptive to new ideas, which could lead to positive outcomes.

Rooster This month might be one of the more challenging ones for you. Be aware that the energy flow is unstable and can affect your work or business. It is not advisable to over-commit your time or finances during this time. Relationships with loved ones may need more attention.

Dog This is a good month for personal contemplations. Some of you may feel like withdrawing from outside activities. Be mindful not to become too introverted, as you may tip the balance and become depressed. Work energy is weak, but there will still be plenty to do, so do not worry too much.

Pig November will not be as quiet as you hope. Expect a busy schedule with work and social engagements. There may be a call for you to share your aspirations and wisdom with people in your circle. Maintaining balance and focus will help you navigate through the month successfully.

11 | NOVEMBER 2024

The Wood Dragon Year

18 Monday
Animal: **Fire Dog**
Flying Star: **2**
Good Day: **Rabbit**
Bad Day: **Dragon**
⚡🏭

19 Tuesday
Animal: **Fire Pig**
Flying Star: **1**
Good Day: **Tiger**
Bad Day: **Snake**

20 Wednesday
Animal: **Earth Rat**
Flying Star: **9**
Good Day: **Ox**
Bad Day: **Horse**
✈️🏠❤️🏭

21 Thursday
Animal: **Earth Ox**
Flying Star: **8**
Good Day: **Rat**
Bad Day: **Goat**

22 Friday
Animal: **Metal Tiger**
Flying Star: **7**
Good Day: **Pig**
Bad Day: **Monkey**
✈️✂️🏠❤️🏭

23 Saturday
Animal: **Metal Rabbit**
Flying Star: **6**
Good Day: **Dog**
Bad Day: **Rooster**
✈️✂️❤️🏠

24 Sunday
Animal: **Water Dragon**
Flying Star: **5**
Good Day: **Rooster**
Bad Day: **Dog**
⚡

11 | NOVEMBER 2024

The Wood Dragon Year

25 Monday
Animal: **Water Snake**
Flying Star: **4**
Good Day: **Monkey**
Bad Day: **Pig**

26 Tuesday
Animal: **Wood Horse**
Flying Star: **3**
Good Day: **Goat**
Bad Day: **Rat**
✈ 🏠 ❤️ 🎬

27 Wednesday
Animal: **Wood Goat**
Flying Star: **2**
Good Day: **Horse**
Bad Day: **Ox**

28 Thursday
Animal: **Fire Monkey**
Flying Star: **1**
Good Day: **Snake**
Bad Day: **Tiger**

29 Friday
Animal: **Fire Rooster**
Flying Star: **9**
Good Day: **Dragon**
Bad Day: **Rabbit**
✈ ✏️ ❤️ 🎬

30 Saturday
Animal: **Earth Dog**
Flying Star: **8**
Good Day: **Rabbit**
Bad Day: **Dragon**
⚡ ❤️ 🎬

1 Sunday
Animal: **Earth Pig**
Flying Star: **7**
Good Day: **Tiger**
Bad Day: **Snake**
✈

DECEMBER 7 - JANUARY 5, 2025, THE MONTH OF THE RAT

RAT Chinese Horoscope 2024: Embrace Opportunities and Balance

The Year 2024 brings a blend of success and challenges for Rats. Diligence and determination will steer them towards favourable outcomes. The Rat's alignment with the Dragon, representing Earth, Water, and Wood elements, ensures a balanced journey. While significant triumphs might not be guaranteed, disasters are averted.

Striving for attainable goals, enhancing skills, and maintaining humility pave the path to success. The Year encourages wisdom-seeking, skill improvement, and readiness for future prosperity.

Career Outlook 2024: Thriving Amid Changes

Rat Career Horoscope 2024 anticipates change and opportunities. The Dragon's energy drives career success, empowering Rats. Competitions arise, but the Dragon's influence fortifies them, encouraging skill display and full potential utilisation. Media, Arts, Science, and Technology sectors flourish.

Love and Relationships: Navigating Transformations

In the realm of love, Rats enjoy harmonious relationships. The Dragon imparts energy, aiding them in overcoming challenges and soaring to new heights. Singles find partners, with positive energy enhancing their allure. Wisdom guides partner selection, urging patience and trust-building.

Married couples flourish, deepening bonds and rekindling passion, promising lasting love.

Financial Outlook: Navigating Prosperity

Financially, 2024 will bring positive outcomes for the Rat. Hard work and resourcefulness yield fruitful results, but cautiousness against unexpected expenses is advised. Prudent investments, guided by the Dragon's support, offer high returns. Expanding ventures or transitioning hobbies to businesses is encouraged.

Health and Wellness: Prioritising Well-being

Health concerns emerge in 2024, requiring attention to the immune system and digestion. Vigilance against injuries is paramount. Natural remedies, exercise, and balanced nutrition maintain vitality. Stress management and mental health care are vital.

Lucky and Unlucky Aspects: Guiding Influences

Lucky colours (Green, Blue, Black), numbers (2, 3), months (May, February, December), and directions (Southeast, Northeast) favour the Rat. Unlucky numbers (5, 9), colours (Brown, Yellow), and months (January, April, August, October) are noted.

The Rat and Dragon Alliance: Harmony and Balance

The Rat's Yin Water aligns with the Dragon's Yang Earth, fostering harmony and balance. Their interaction symbolises interpersonal skills, career, and monetary growth. The Rat prospers within the Dragon's working environment, turning intelligence into financial success. Mutual attraction and sacrifice yield prosperity.

2024: Rat's Encounter with the Green Dragon

The Year of the Green Dragon ushers in positive transformations for the Rat. Careers thrive due to combined elements. Fire symbolises wealth and income, offering financial stability. Love blossoms as the Rat-Dragon connection enhances charm. Social networks expand, benefiting both personal and professional spheres.

Balance, Success, and Harmony

2024 aligns success, challenges, and harmony for the Rat. Embracing opportunities, navigating change, and maintaining well-being leads to a fruitful year. The Rat-Dragon synergy enhances career, finance, and love prospects, promising a balanced journey filled with achievements.

DECEMBER Flying Star 4, Romance, Wisdom, and Scholarly Flourish

December's monthly energy is of romance, wisdom, and a scholarly flourish, with the Flying Star 4 emerging as a harmonious melody that resonates with a tapestry of attributes within the cosmic symphony of celestial energies. It brings romance, intelligence, talent, and wisdom, weaving threads of fame, promotion, and academic brilliance into the fabric of existence. Often referred to as the Peach Blossom Star, it exudes an aura of beauty, knowledge, and learning that enriches the lives it touches.

As the energies of Flying Star 4 infuse the surroundings, an enchanting dance of harmony and happiness envelops love relationships. Its benevolent influence sets the stage for meaningful and fulfilling connections, making it especially promising for singles seeking the blossoming of love and marriage. This star's tender touch fosters an environment where the seeds of romance can flourish, yielding companionship and a profound depth of emotion.

Beyond matters of the heart, Flying Star 4 bestows its blessings upon individuals with a literary, artistic, or creative inclination. For educators, lecturers, artists, writers, and researchers, its presence brings positive outcomes, hinting at the promise of advancement and recognition. Students, too, are enveloped by its embrace, with better luck in examinations and increased success in applications for esteemed educational institutions.

To nurture the flames of love and romance, couples are urged to adorn their spaces with symbols of affection. Placing two Rose Quartz crystals near or beneath the bed is a beacon of love's energy. Love symbols such as Mandarin Ducks, Wish-fulfilling Birds, or embracing figurines are tangible reminders of the shared tender connection.

For those seeking to amplify their academic fortunes, Flying Star 4 beckons them to embrace the scholarly realm. The display of Chinese ink brushes or artistic renderings, tiered pagodas, revered Chinese saint Luohan, or the revered three Star Gods can harmoniously intertwine with this star's essence. Through these tokens, the path to academic excellence finds itself illuminated by the benevolent glow of Flying Star 4.

Pertaining to the Luo Shu or Bagua school of Feng Shui, the annual Flying Star 4 sits in the North-West sector for 2024; this sector represents the man of the house and signifies influential benefactors, mentors, and helpful people.

The North West belongs to the element of Metal; in Chinese culture, metal also signifies gold. So, this is also a pocket of family wealth. To tap into and enhance, use metal décor items, coloured objects, bells or wind chimes. The three Star Gods represent health, wealth and longevity and are excellent used in a home's main living area to benefit all occupants.

12 | DECEMBER 2024

The Wood Dragon Year

2 Monday
Animal: **Metal Rat**
Flying Star: **6**
Good Day: **Ox**
Bad Day: **Horse**
🏠✈️✂️❤️🎬

3 Tuesday
Animal: **Metal Ox**
Flying Star: **5**
Good Day: **Rat**
Bad Day: **Goat**
⚡

4 Wednesday
Animal: **Water Tiger**
Flying Star: **4**
Good Day: **Pig**
Bad Day: **Monkey**
✈️✂️🏠🎬

5 Thursday
Animal: **Water Rabbit**
Flying Star: **3**
Good Day: **Dog**
Bad Day: **Rooster**
✈️✂️🏠❤️🎬

6 Friday
Animal: **Wood Dragon**
Flying Star: **2**
Good Day: **Rooster**
Bad Day: **Dog**
🎬

7 Saturday
Animal: **Wood Snake**
Flying Star: **1**
Good Day: **Monkey**
Bad Day: **Pig**
🏠❤️🎬

8 Sunday
Animal: **Fire Horse**
Flying Star: **9**
Good Day: **Goat**
Bad Day: **Rat**

DECEMBER MONTHLY CHINESE ZODIAC OVERVIEW

Rat Energy resurges this month, allowing you to enjoy the year-end season. Life transitions to a less demanding pace, providing opportunities to cherish moments with loved ones. Pay attention to the well-being of elderly family members; extra help may be needed to balance the situation.

Ox The positive energy of this month enhances your mind and spirit. Anticipate a busy month ahead, marked by work activities that will keep you occupied. Social engagements such as travel, lunches, and parties demand a balance between work and leisure.

Tiger You have reached a juncture where positive transformations are set to unfold in your life, marking the beginning of a new journey. For now, you should strive to enhance collaboration with others to achieve your objectives and maintain harmonious interpersonal relationships.

Rabbit This is a hectic and competitive month. Having confidence in your decisions and being resolute is crucial, as this approach will grant you control over various situations. To maintain a harmonious work environment, it is best to avoid arguments with superiors. Rash money decisions should be avoided.

Dragon During this dynamic month, you can maximise your enjoyment by maintaining physical well-being and a harmonious activity equilibrium. Social activities will fill your calendar quickly. Staying energetically healthy will enable you to make the most of this time.

Snake The energy this month is supportive, and it will assist you in finding stability and boosting your self-assurance. It also offers an opportunity to enhance connections and establish a stronger foundation with family and loved ones. Work energy is vital, and increased activities are indicated.

Horse While the energy might experience a slight fluctuation, you can still anticipate a relatively decent month ahead. Be prepared for a fast-paced environment at work and keep up with the momentum. Clear communication is crucial this month, as it can help prevent unnecessary complications. As personal safety is important this month, try to avoid rushing around, especially with tasks involving the stairs.

Goat As the energy calms down, it is essential to trust your inner guidance and intuition. Recognise that the current point is still supportive and guiding you forward. Keep your focus on your long-term goals and aspirations. This is a period when your steadfastness and determination will contribute to your success.

12 | DECEMBER 2024

The Wood Dragon Year

9 Monday
Animal: **Fire Goat**
Flying Star: **8**
Good Day: **Horse**
Bad Day: **Ox**
🏭

10 Tuesday
Animal: **Earth Monkey**
Flying Star: **7**
Good Day: **Snake**
Bad Day: **Tiger**

11 Wednesday
Animal: **Earth Rooster**
Flying Star: **6**
Good Day: **Dragon**
Bad Day: **Rabbit**

12 Thursday
Animal: **Metal Dog**
Flying Star: **5**
Good Day: **Rabbit**
Bad Day: **Dragon**
⚡🏭

13 Friday
Animal: **Metal Pig**
Flying Star: **4**
Good Day: **Tiger**
Bad Day: **Snake**
🏭

14 Saturday
Animal: **Water Rat**
Flying Star: **3**
Good Day: **Ox**
Bad Day: **Horse**

15 Sunday
Animal: **Water Ox**
Flying Star: **2**
Good Day: **Rat**
Bad Day: **Goat**
✈️💇❤️🏠

Monkey The pace of this month will be swift, and you need to maintain your focus. As the month progresses, be prepared for new opportunities that could offer you fresh avenues for growth and advancement. Look after your well-being, especially if you have been experiencing fatigue.

Rooster This month holds the potential for success, and you will feel a well-deserved sense of accomplishment and satisfaction. Work continues to be demanding, and it is wise to maintain control over your actions and decisions for better results. Financially, this is an average month.

Dog December brings positive energy, and your overall vitality will be enhanced. Embrace the optimistic power around you and use this time to plan to achieve your goals and aspirations. Stay open to new possibilities that come your way.

Pig Embrace the lively energy for a more enjoyable month ahead. If something in your environment is causing distress, take proactive steps to fix it before mid-month. Money energy is positive. Family and friends will be warm and supportive throughout this celebrative season. Enjoy the positive vibes and make the most of this joyous time.

12 | DECEMBER 2024

The Wood Dragon Year

16 Monday
Animal: **Wood Tiger**
Flying Star: **1**
Good Day: **Pig**
Bad Day: **Monkey**

17 Tuesday
Animal: **Wood Rabbit**
Flying Star: **9**
Good Day: **Dog**
Bad Day: **Rooster**

18 Wednesday
Animal: **Fire Dragon**
Flying Star: **8**
Good Day: **Rooster**
Bad Day: **Dog**

19 Thursday
Animal: **Fire Snake**
Flying Star: **7**
Good Day: **Monkey**
Bad Day: **Pig**

20 Friday
Animal: **Earth Horse**
Flying Star: **6**
Good Day: **Goat**
Bad Day: **Rat**

21 Saturday
Animal: **Earth Goat**
Flying Star: **5/5**
Good Day: **Horse**
Bad Day: **Ox**

22 Sunday
Animal: **Earth Monkey**
Flying Star: **6**
Good Day: **Snake**
Bad Day: **Tiger**

ACTIVATING FENG SHUI IN THE GARDEN

Each orientation possesses a distinct element. Employ the productive cycle to amplify the influence of each element. Utilise colours symbolically to manifest the essence of these elements.

12 | DECEMBER 2024

The Wood Dragon Year

23 Monday
Animal: **Metal Rooster**
Flying Star: **7**
Good Day: **Dragon**
Bad Day: **Rabbit**

24 Tuesday
Animal: **Metal Dog**
Flying Star: **8**
Good Day: **Rabbit**
Bad Day: **Dragon**
✈️🎬

25 Wednesday
Animal: **Water Pig**
Flying Star: **9**
Good Day: **Tiger**
Bad Day: **Snake**

26 Thursday
Animal: **Water Rat**
Flying Star: **1**
Good Day: **Ox**
Bad Day: **Horse**

27 Friday
Animal: **Wood Ox**
Flying Star: **2**
Good Day: **Rat**
Bad Day: **Goat**
✈️✂️❤️🎬

28 Saturday
Animal: **Wood Tiger**
Flying Star: **3**
Good Day: **Pig**
Bad Day: **Monkey**
✈️✂️

29 Sunday
Animal: **Fire Rabbit**
Flying Star: **4**
Good Day: **Dog**
Bad Day: **Rooster**

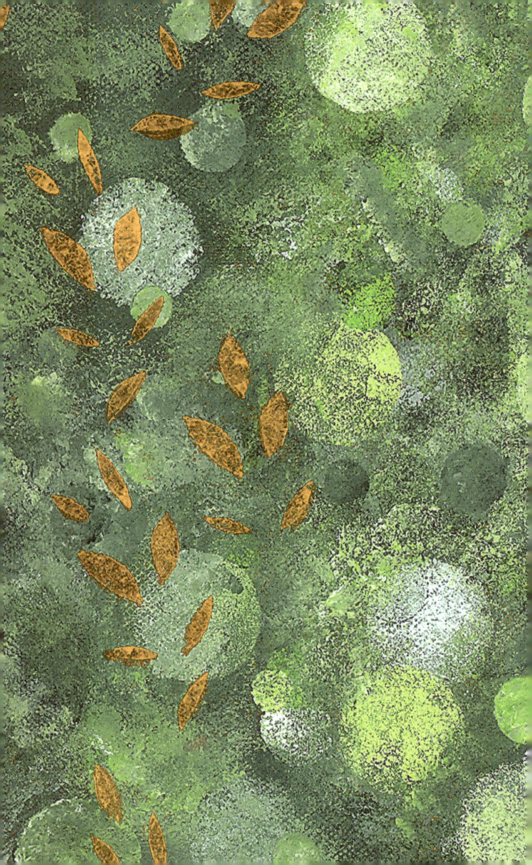

12 | DECEMBER 2024

The Wood Dragon Year

30 Monday
Animal: **Fire Dragon**
Flying Star: **5**
Good Day: **Rooster**
Bad Day: **Dog**

31 Tuesday
Animal: **Earth Snake**
Flying Star: **6**
Good Day: **Monkey**
Bad Day: **Pig**

1 Wednesday (New Year Day)
Animal: **Earth Horse**
Flying Star: **7**
Good Day: **Dog**
Bad Day: **Rat**

2 Thursday
Animal: **Metal Goat**
Flying Star: **8**
Good Day: **Dog**
Bad Day: **Ox**

3 Friday
Animal: **Metal Monkey**
Flying Star: **9**
Good Day: **Dragon**
Bad Day: **Tiger**

4 Saturday
Animal: **Water Rooster**
Flying Star: **1**
Good Day: **Dragon**
Bad Day: **Rabbit**

5 Sunday
Animal: **Water Dog**
Flying Star: **2**
Good Day: **Monkey**
Bad Day: **Dragon**

Your Kua Number

YEAR OF BIRTH	ANIMAL SIGN	HEAVENLY STEM	BORN BETWEEN...	MEN	WOMEN
1900	Rat	Metal	Jan 31, 1900-Feb 18, 1901	1	5
1901	Ox	Metal	Feb 19,1901 - Feb 7, 1902	9	6
1902	Tiger	Water	Feb 8, 1902-Jan 28, 1903	8	7
1903	Rabbit	Water	Jan 29,1903-Feb 28, 1904	7	8
1904	Dragon	Wood	Feb 16,1904- Feb 3,1905	6	9
1905	Snake	Wood	Feb 4, 1905-Jan 24, 1906	5	1
1906	Horse	Fire	Jan 25,1906-Feb 12,1907	4	2
1907	Goat	Fire	Feb 13, 1907- Feb 1, 1908	3	3
1908	Monkey	Earth	Feb 2,1908-Jan 21, 1909	2	4
1909	Rooster	Earth	Jan 22,1909- Feb 9,1910	1	5
1910	Dog	Metal	Feb 10, 1910-Jan 29,1911	9	6
1911	Pig	Metal	Jan 30,1911 - Feb 17,1912	8	7
1912	Rat	Water	Feb 18, 1912-Feb 5, 1913	7	8
1913	Ox	Water	Feb 6, 1913-Jan 25, 1914	6	9
1914	Tiger	Wood	Jan 26,1914- Feb 13, 1915	5	1
1915	Rabbit	Wood	Feb 14,1915-Feb 2,1916	4	2
1916	Dragon	Fire	Feb 3,1916-Jan 22,1917	3	3
1917	Snake	Fire	Jan 23, 1917- Feb 10, 1918	2	4
1918	Horse	Earth	Feb 11,1918-Jan 31, 1919	1	5
1919	Goat	Earth	Feb 1,1919-Feb 19, 1920	9	6
1920	Monkey	Metal	Feb 20, 1920-Feb 7, 1921	8	7
1921	Rooster	Metal	Feb 8,1921 - Jan 27, 1922	7	8
1922	Dog	Water	Jan 28, 1922-Feb 15, 1923	6	9
1923	Pig	Water	Feb 16,1923- Feb 4, 1924	5	1
1924	Rat	Wood	Feb 5, 1924-Jan 23, 1925	4	2
1925	Ox	Wood	Jan 24, 1925- Feb 12, 1926	3	3
1926	Tiger	Fire	Feb 13,1926- Feb 1,1927	2	4
1927	Rabbit	Fire	Feb 2, 1927-Jan 22, 1928	1	5

YEAR OF BIRTH	ANIMAL SIGN	HEAVENLY STEM	BORN BETWEEN...	MEN	WOMEN
1928	Dragon	Earth	Jan 23,1928- Feb 9, 1929	9	6
1929	Snake	Earth	Feb 10,1929 - Jan 29,1930	8	7
1930	Horse	Metal	Jan 30,1930- Feb 16 1931	7	8
1931	Goat	Metal	Feb 17,1931 - Feb 5, 1932	6	9
1932	Monkey	Water	Feb 6, 1932-Jan 25,1933	5	1
1933	Rooster	Water	Jan 26, 1933-Feb 13, 1934	4	2
1934	Dog	Wood	Feb 14,1934- Feb 3,1935	3	3
1935	Pig	Wood	Feb 4, 1935-Jan 23, 1936	2	4
1936	Rat	Fire	Jan 24, 1936- Feb 10,1937	1	5
1937	Ox	Fire	Feb 11,1937-Jan 30,1938	9	6
1938	Tiger	Earth	Jan 31,1938-Feb 18, 1939	8	7
1939	Rabbit	Earth	Feb 19, 1939- Feb 7, 1940	7	8
1940	Dragon	Metal	Feb 8, 1940-Jan 26, 1941	6	9
1941	Snake	Metal	Jan 27, 1941 - Feb 14, 1942	5	1
1942	Horse	Water	Feb 15, 1942 - Feb 4,1943	4	2
1943	Goat	Water	Feb 5, 1943-Jan 24, 1944	3	3
1944	Monkey	Wood	Jan 25,1944-Feb 12,1945	2	4
1945	Rooster	Wood	Feb 13, 1945 - Feb 1, 1946	1	5
1946	Dog	Fire	Feb 2, 1946-Jan 21, 1947	9	6
1947	Pig	Fire	Jan 22, 1947-Feb 9, 1948	8	7
1948	Rat	Earth	Feb 10, 1948-Jan 28, 1949	7	8
1949	Ox	Earth	Jan 29, 1949-Feb 16, 1950	6	9
1950	Tiger	Metal	Feb 17 1950- Feb 5,1951	5	1
1951	Rabbit	Metal	Feb 6, 1951 - Jan 26 1952	4	2
1952	Dragon	Water	Jan 27,1952 - Feb 13,1953	3	3
1953	Snake	Water	Feb 14, 1953- Feb 2, 1954	2	4
1954	Horse	Wood	Feb 3, 1954-Jan 23, 1955	1	5
1955	Goat	Wood	Jan 24, 1955-Feb 11, 1956	9	6
1956	Monkey	Fire	Feb 12,1956-Jan 30, 1957	8	7
1957	Rooster	Fire	Jan 31, 1957-Feb 17, 1958	7	8
1958	Dog	Earth	Feb 18, 1958-Feb 7 1959	6	9
1959	Pig	Earth	Feb 8, 1959-Jan 27, 1960	5	1

YEAR OF BIRTH	ANIMAL SIGN	HEAVENLY STEM	BORN BETWEEN...	MEN	WOMEN
1960	Rat	Metal	Jan 28, 1960 - Feb 14, 1961	4	2
1961	Ox	Metal	Feb 15, 1961 - Feb 4, 1962	3	3
1962	Tiger	Water	Feb 5, 1962 - Jan 24, 1963	2	4
1963	Rabbit	Water	Jan 25, 1963- Feb 12 1964	1	5
1964	Dragon	Wood	Feb 13, 1964-Feb 1,1965	9	6
1965	Snake	Wood	Feb 2, 1965-Jan 20, 1966	8	7
1966	Horse	Fire	Jan 21,1966-Feb 8,1967	7	8
1967	Goat	Fire	Feb 9,1967-Jan 29,1968	6	9
1968	Monkey	Earth	Jan 30, 1968-Feb 16, 1969	5	1
1969	Rooster	Earth	Feb 17, 1969-Feb 5, 1970	4	2
1970	Dog	Metal	Feb 6, 1970-Jan 26,1971	3	3
1971	Pig	Metal	Jan 27, 1971 - Feb 14, 1972	2	4
1972	Rat	Water	Feb 15, 1972-Feb 2, 1973	1	5
1973	Ox	Water	Feb 3, 1973-Jan 22, 1974	9	6
1974	Tiger	Wood	Jan 23, 1974-Feb 10, 1975	8	7
1975	Rabbit	Wood	Feb 11, 1975 - Jan 30, 1976	7	8
1976	Dragon	Fire	Jan 31, 1976-Feb 17 1977	6	9
1977	Snake	Fire	Feb 18,1977- Feb 6, 1978	5	1
1978	Horse	Earth	Feb 7, 1978 - Jan 27, 1979	4	2
1979	Goat	Earth	Jan 28, 1979 - Feb 15, 1980	3	3
1980	Monkey	Metal	Feb 16, 1980- Feb 4, 1981	2	4
1981	Rooster	Metal	Feb 5, 1981 - Jan 24, 1982	1	5
1982	Dog	Water	Jan 25, 1982-Feb12, 1983	9	6
1983	Pig	Water	Feb 13,1983- Feb 1,1984	8	7
1984	Rat	Wood	Feb 2,1984- Feb 19, 1985	7	8
1985	Ox	Wood	Feb 20, 1985-Feb 8, 1986	6	9
1986	Tiger	Fire	Feb 9, 1986-Jan 28, 1987	5	1
1987	Rabbit	Fire	Jan 29, 1987- Feb 16, 1988	4	2
1988	Dragon	Earth	Feb 17, 1988- Feb 5, 1989	3	3
1989	Snake	Earth	Feb 6, 1989-Jan 26, 1990	2	4
1990	Horse	Metal	Jan 27,1990 - Feb 14,1991	1	5
1991	Goat	Metal	Feb 15, 1991 - Feb 3, 1992	9	6

YEAR OF BIRTH	ANIMAL SIGN	HEAVENLY STEM	BORN BETWEEN...	MEN	WOMEN
1992	Monkey	Water	Feb 4, 1992-Jan 22, 1993	8	7
1993	Rooster	Water	Jan 23, 1993 - Feb 9, 1994	7	8
1994	Dog	Wood	Feb 10, 1994-Jan 30, 1995	6	9
1995	Pig	Wood	Jan 31, 1995-Feb 18, 1996	5	1
1996	Rat	Fire	Feb 19, 1996 - Feb 6, 1997	4	2
1997	Ox	Fire	Feb 7, 1997 - Jan 27, 1998	3	3
1998	Tiger	Earth	Jan 28, 1998 - Feb 15, 1999	2	4
1999	Rabbit	Earth	Feb 16, 1999-Feb 4, 2000	1	5
2000	Dragon	Metal	Feb 5, 2000 - Jan 23, 2001	9	6
2001	Snake	Metal	Jan 24, 2001 - Feb 11, 2002	8	7
2002	Horse	Water	Feb 12, 2002-Jan 31, 2003	7	8
2003	Goat	Water	Feb 1, 2003 - Jan 21, 2004	6	9
2004	Monkey	Wood	Jan 22, 2004 - Feb 8, 2005	5	1
2005	Rooster	Wood	Feb 9, 2005 - Jan 28, 2006	4	2
2006	Dog	Fire	Jan 29, 2006-Feb 17 2007	3	3
2007	Pig	Fire	Feb 18, 2007 - Feb 6, 2008	2	4
2008	Rat	Earth	Feb 7 2008 - Jan 25, 2009	1	5
2009	Ox	Earth	Jan 26, 2009 - Feb 13, 2010	9	6
2010	Tiger	Metal	Feb 14, 2010-Feb 2, 2011	8	7
2011	Rabbit	Metal	Feb 3, 2011 - Jan 22, 2012	7	8
2012	Dragon	Water	Jan 23, 2012-Feb 9, 2013	6	9
2013	Snake	Water	Feb 10, 2013-Jan 30, 2014	5	1
2014	Horse	Wood	Jan 31, 2014-Feb 18, 2015	4	2
2015	Goat	Wood	Feb 19, 2015-Feb 7, 2016	3	3
2016	Monkey	Fire	Feb 8, 2016-Jan 27, 2017	2	4
2017	Rooster	Fire	Jan 28, 2017-Feb 15, 2018	1	5
2018	Dog	Earth	Feb 16, 2018-Feb 4, 2019	9	6
2019	Pig	Earth	Feb 5, 2019 - Jan 24, 2020	8	7
2020	Rat	Metal	Jan 25, 2020 - Feb 11, 2021	7	8
2021	Ox	Metal	Feb 12, 2021 - Jan 31, 2022	6	9
2022	Tiger	Water	Feb 1, 2022-Jan 21, 2023	5	1
2023	Rabbit	Water	Jan 22, 2023 - Feb 9, 2024	4	2

YEAR OF BIRTH	ANIMAL SIGN	HEAVENLY STEM	BORN BETWEEN...	MEN	WOMEN
2024	Dragon	Wood	Feb 10, 2024-Jan 28, 2025	3	3
2025	Snake	Wood	Jan 29, 2025-Feb 16, 2026	2	4
2026	Horse	Fire	Feb 17, 2026 - Feb 5, 2027	1	5
2027	Goat	Fire	Feb 6, 2027 - Jan 25, 2028	9	6
2028	Monkey	Earth	Jan 26, 2028 - Feb 12, 2029	8	7
2029	Rooster	Earth	Feb 13, 2029-Feb 2, 2030	7	8
2030	Dog	Metal	Feb 3, 2030 - Jan 22, 2031	6	9
2031	Pig	Metal	Jan 23, 2031 - Feb 10, 2032	5	1
2032	Rat	Water	Feb 11, 2032-Jan 30, 2033	4	2
2033	Ox	Water	Jan 31, 2033- Feb 18, 2034	3	3
2034	Tiger	Wood	Feb 19, 2034 - Feb 7 2035	2	4
2035	Rabbit	Wood	Feb 8, 2035 - Jan 27, 2036	1	5
2036	Dragon	Fire	Jan 28, 2036 - Feb 14, 2037	9	6
2037	Snake	Fire	Feb 15, 2037- Feb 3, 2038	8	7
2038	Horse	Earth	Feb 4, 2038 - Jan 23, 2039	7	8
2039	Goat	Earth	Jan 24, 2039 - Feb 11, 2040	6	9
2040	Monkey	Metal	Feb 12, 2040-Jan 31, 2041	5	1
2041	Rooster	Metal	Feb 1, 2041 - Jan 21, 2042	4	2
2042	Dog	Water	Jan 22, 2042 - Feb 9, 2043	3	3
2043	Pig	Water	Feb 10, 2043-Jan 29, 2044	2	4
2044	Rat	Wood	Jan 30, 2044-Feb 16, 2045	1	5
2045	Ox	Wood	Feb 17 2045 - Feb 5, 2046	9	6
2046	Tiger	Fire	Feb 6, 2046 - Jan 25, 2047	8	7
2047	Rabbit	Fire	Jan 26, 2047 - Feb 13, 2048	7	8
2048	Dragon	Earth	Feb 14, 2048 - Feb 1, 2049	6	9
2049	Snake	Earth	Feb 2, 2049 - Jan 22, 2050	5	1
2050	Horse	Metal	Jan 23, 2050 - Feb 11, 2051	4	2
2051	Goat	Metal	Feb 12, 2051 - Jan 31, 2052	3	3
2052	Monkey	Water	Feb 1, 2052-Feb 18, 2053	2	4
2053	Rooster	Water	Feb 19, 2053 - Feb 7, 2054	1	5
2054	Dog	Wood	Feb 8, 2054 - Jan 27, 2055	9	6

Auspicious and Inauspicious Directions
Based on your Kua Number

Position yourself in a favourble orientation for significant activities. Whether seating a deal, engaging in work or meals, delivering a presentation, attending a learning session, or even during sleep, ensure your head is directed towards a positive angle. Steer clear of unfavourable orientations whenever possible.

Auspicious Directions:

Kua Number	Sheng Chi (Best Direction)	Tien Yi (Health Direction)	Nien Yen (Romance Direction)	Fu Wei (Personal Growth Direction)
1	Southeast	East	South	North
2	Northeast	West	Northwest	Southwest
3	South	North	Southeast	East
4	North	South	East	Southeast
6	West	Northeast	Southwest	Northwest
7	Northwest	Southwest	Northeast	West
8	Southwest	Northwest	West	Northeast
9	East	Southeast	North	South

Inauspicious Directions:

Kua Number	Ho Hai (Unlucky)	Wu Kwei (Five Ghosts)	Lui Sha (Six Killings)	Chueh Ming (Total Loss)
1	West	Northeast	Northwest	Southwest
2	East	Southeast	South	North
3	Southwest	Northwest	Northeast	West
4	Northwest	Southwest	West	Northeast
6	Southeast	East	North	South
7	North	South	Southeast	East
8	South	North	East	Southeast
9	Northeast	West	Southwest	Northwest

2024

JANUARY
MO	1	8	15	22	29
TU	2	9	16	23	30
WE	3	10	17	24	31
TH	4	11	18	25	
FR	5	12	19	26	
SA	6	13	20	27	
SU	7	14	21	28	

FEBRUARY
MO		5	12	19	26
TU		6	13	20	27
WE		7	14	21	28
TH	1	8	15	22	29
FR	2	9	16	23	
SA	3	10	17	24	
SU	4	11	18	25	

MARCH
MO		4	11	18	25
TU		5	12	19	26
WE		6	13	20	27
TH		7	14	21	28
FR	1	8	15	22	29
SA	2	9	16	23	30
SU	3	10	17	24	31

APRIL
MO	1	8	15	22	29
TU	2	9	16	23	30
WE	3	10	17	24	
TH	4	11	18	25	
FR	5	12	19	26	
SA	6	13	20	27	
SU	7	14	21	28	

MAY
MO		6	13	20	27
TU		7	14	21	28
WE	1	8	15	22	29
TH	2	9	16	23	30
FR	3	10	17	24	31
SA	4	11	18	25	
SU	5	12	19	26	

JUNE
MO		3	10	17	24
TU		4	11	18	25
WE		5	12	19	26
TH		6	13	20	27
FR		7	14	21	28
SA	1	8	15	22	29
SU	2	9	16	23	30

JULY
MO	1	8	15	22	29
TU	2	9	16	23	30
WE	3	10	17	24	31
TH	4	11	18	25	
FR	5	12	19	26	
SA	6	13	20	27	
SU	7	14	21	28	

AUGUST
MO		5	12	19	26
TU		6	13	20	27
WE		7	14	21	28
TH	1	8	15	22	29
FR	2	9	16	23	30
SA	3	10	17	24	31
SU	4	11	18	25	

SEPTEMBER
MO	30	2	9	16	23
TU		3	10	17	24
WE		4	11	18	25
TH		5	12	19	26
FR		6	13	20	27
SA		7	14	21	28
SU	1	8	15	22	29

OCTOBER
MO		7	14	21	28
TU	1	8	15	22	29
WE	2	9	16	23	30
TH	3	10	17	24	31
FR	4	11	18	25	
SA	5	12	19	26	
SU	6	13	20	27	

NOVEMBER
MO		4	11	18	25
TU		5	12	19	26
WE		6	13	20	27
TH		7	14	21	28
FR	1	8	15	22	29
SA	2	9	16	23	30
SU	3	10	17	24	

DECEMBER
MO	30	2	9	16	23
TU	31	3	10	17	24
WE		4	11	18	25
TH		5	12	19	26
FR		6	13	20	27
SA		7	14	21	28
SU	1	8	15	22	29

2025

	JANUARY			
MO		6	13	20	27
TU		7	14	21	28
WE	1	8	15	22	29
TH	2	9	16	23	30
FR	3	10	17	24	31
SA	4	11	18	25
SU	5	12	19	26

	FEBRUARY			
MO		3	10	17	24
TU		4	11	18	25
WE		5	12	19	26
TH		6	13	20	27
FR		7	14	21	28
SA	1	8	15	22
SU	2	9	16	23

	MARCH				
MO	31	3	10	17	24
TU		4	11	18	25
WE		5	12	19	26
TH		6	13	20	27
FR		7	14	21	28
SA	1	8	15	22	29
SU	2	9	16	23	30

	APRIL			
MO		7	14	21	28
TU	1	8	15	22	29
WE	2	9	16	23	30
TH	3	10	17	24
FR	4	11	18	25
SA	5	12	19	26
SU	6	13	20	27

	MAY			
MO		5	12	19	26
TU		6	13	20	27
WE		7	14	21	28
TH	1	8	15	22	29
FR	2	9	16	23	30
SA	3	10	17	24	31
SU	4	11	18	25

	JUNE				
MO	30	2	9	16	23
TU		3	10	17	24
WE		4	11	18	25
TH		5	12	19	26
FR		6	13	20	27
SA		7	14	21	28
SU	1	8	15	22	29

	JULY			
MO		7	14	21	28
TU	1	8	15	22	29
WE	2	9	16	23	30
TH	3	10	17	24	31
FR	4	11	18	25
SA	5	12	19	26
SU	6	13	20	27

	AUGUST			
MO		4	11	18	25
TU		5	12	19	26
WE		6	13	20	27
TH		7	14	21	28
FR	1	8	15	22	29
SA	2	9	16	23	30
SU	3	10	17	24	31

	SEPTEMBER			
MO	1	8	15	22	29
TU	2	9	16	23	30
WE	3	10	17	24
TH	4	11	18	25
FR	5	12	19	26
SA	6	13	20	27
SU	7	14	21	28

	OCTOBER			
MO		6	13	20	27
TU		7	14	21	28
WE	1	8	15	22	29
TH	2	9	16	23	30
FR	3	10	17	24	31
SA	4	11	18	25
SU	5	12	19	26

	NOVEMBER			
MO		3	10	17	24
TU		4	11	18	25
WE		5	12	19	26
TH		6	13	20	27
FR		7	14	21	28
SA	1	8	15	22	29
SU	2	9	16	23	30

	DECEMBER				
MO	1	8	15	22	29
TU	2	9	16	23	30
WE	3	10	17	24	31
TH	4	11	18	25
FR	5	12	19	26
SA	6	13	20	27
SU	7	14	21	28

2024 Year Planner

DAY	JANUARY	FEBRUARY	MARCH
MONDAY	1		
TUESDAY	2		
WEDNESDAY	3		
THURSDAY	4	1	
FRIDAY	5	2	1
SATURDAY	6	3	2
SUNDAY	7	4	3
MONDAY	8	5	4
TUESDAY	9	6	5
WEDNESDAY	10	7	6
THURSDAY	11	8	7
FRIDAY	12	9	8
SATURDAY	13	10	9
SUNDAY	14	11	10
MONDAY	15	12	11
TUESDAY	16	13	12
WEDNESDAY	17	14	13
THURSDAY	18	15	14
FRIDAY	19	16	15
SATURDAY	20	17	16
SUNDAY	21	18	17
MONDAY	22	19	18
TUESDAY	23	20	19
WEDNESDAY	24	21	20
THURSDAY	25	22	21
FRIDAY	26	23	22
SATURDAY	27	24	23
SUNDAY	28	25	24
MONDAY	29	26	25
TUESDAY	30	27	26
WEDNESDAY	31	28	27
THURSDAY		29	28
FRIDAY			29
SATURDAY			30
SUNDAY			31
MONDAY			
TUESDAY			

2024 Year Planner

APRIL	MAY	JUNE	DAY
1			MONDAY
2			TUESDAY
3	1		WEDNESDAY
4	2		THURSDAY
5	3		FRIDAY
6	4	1	SATURDAY
7	5	2	SUNDAY
8	6	3	MONDAY
9	7	4	TUESDAY
10	8	5	WEDNESDAY
11	9	6	THURSDAY
12	10	7	FRIDAY
13	11	8	SATURDAY
14	12	9	SUNDAY
15	13	10	MONDAY
16	14	11	TUESDAY
17	15	12	WEDNESDAY
18	16	13	THURSDAY
19	17	14	FRIDAY
20	18	15	SATURDAY
21	19	16	SUNDAY
22	20	17	MONDAY
23	21	18	TUESDAY
24	22	19	WEDNESDAY
25	23	20	THURSDAY
26	24	21	FRIDAY
27	25	22	SATURDAY
28	26	23	SUNDAY
29	27	24	MONDAY
30	28	25	TUESDAY
	29	26	WEDNESDAY
	30	27	THURSDAY
	31	28	FRIDAY
		29	SATURDAY
		30	SUNDAY
			MONDAY
			TUESDAY

2024 Year Planner

DAY	JULY	AUGUST	SEPTEMBER
MONDAY	1		
TUESDAY	2		
WEDNESDAY	3		
THURSDAY	4	1	
FRIDAY	5	2	
SATURDAY	6	3	
SUNDAY	7	4	1
MONDAY	8	5	2
TUESDAY	9	6	3
WEDNESDAY	10	7	4
THURSDAY	11	8	5
FRIDAY	12	9	6
SATURDAY	13	10	7
SUNDAY	14	11	8
MONDAY	15	12	9
TUESDAY	16	13	10
WEDNESDAY	17	14	11
THURSDAY	18	15	12
FRIDAY	19	16	13
SATURDAY	20	17	14
SUNDAY	21	18	15
MONDAY	22	19	16
TUESDAY	23	20	17
WEDNESDAY	24	21	18
THURSDAY	25	22	19
FRIDAY	26	23	20
SATURDAY	27	24	21
SUNDAY	28	25	22
MONDAY	29	26	23
TUESDAY	30	27	24
WEDNESDAY	31	28	25
THURSDAY		29	26
FRIDAY		30	27
SATURDAY		31	28
SUNDAY			29
MONDAY			30
TUESDAY			

2024 Year Planner

OCTOBER	NOVEMBER	DECEMBER	DAY
			MONDAY
1			TUESDAY
2			WEDNESDAY
3			THURSDAY
4	1		FRIDAY
5	2		SATURDAY
6	3	1	SUNDAY
7	4	2	MONDAY
8	5	3	TUESDAY
9	6	4	WEDNESDAY
10	7	5	THURSDAY
11	8	6	FRIDAY
12	9	7	SATURDAY
13	10	8	SUNDAY
14	11	9	MONDAY
15	12	10	TUESDAY
16	13	11	WEDNESDAY
17	14	12	THURSDAY
18	15	13	FRIDAY
19	16	14	SATURDAY
20	17	15	SUNDAY
21	18	16	MONDAY
22	19	17	TUESDAY
23	20	18	WEDNESDAY
24	21	19	THURSDAY
25	22	20	FRIDAY
26	23	21	SATURDAY
27	24	22	SUNDAY
28	25	23	MONDAY
29	26	24	TUESDAY
30	27	25	WEDNESDAY
31	28	26	THURSDAY
	29	27	FRIDAY
	30	28	SATURDAY
		29	SUNDAY
		30	MONDAY
		31	TUESDAY

BEGINNERS FENG SHUI

'EASY TIPS TO ENHANCE EVERYDAY LIVING'

Feng Shui, the "art of placement and manipulation of energy".

Embark on a transformative journey into the ancient art of Feng Shui with "Beginners Feng Shui." This guide, meticulously crafted by Michele Castle, distils two decades of expertise into a comprehensive beginner's manual. Uncover the secrets of Chi energy flow and the art of placement to bring balance, harmony, and prosperity to your living space. Whether you're a novice eager to learn or seeking inspiration for your next home renovation, this book is the perfect companion. Delve into health, wealth, relationship, and career strategies through symbolism, placement techniques, and the use of colour. Elevate your understanding of Feng Shui with this insightful guide, ideal for learning enthusiasts and those looking to enhance their homes.

Available Audible, Ebook or hardcover https://amzn.to/3uCoMOU

DISCOVER THE POWER OF PERIOD 9 FENG SHUI AND CHINESE ASTROLOGY 2024 – 2044

Explore the captivating world of Feng Shui and Chinese Astrology with an Audible, Ebook or hardcover copy of "Period 9 Feng Shui and Chinese Astrology 2024 – 2044." Authored by Michele Castle, a dedicated expert in Feng Shui, this book unravels the mystique of Period 9, a twenty-year cycle from February 4, 2024, to February 3, 2044. Discover the transformative power of the Fire Element, fostering personal growth, creativity, and innovation. Delve into tailored Feng Shui techniques, aligning with the energies of Period 9, and envision your dreams becoming reality. Navigate cosmic influences with flying stars charts and dynamic period energy. Join a vibrant community of seekers ready to explore and connect on this enlightening journey. Michele Castle, a trailblazer in Feng Shui, invites you to unlock the secrets of Period 9 for a life-changing odyssey toward unprecedented success and prosperity. For inquiries or courses, contact

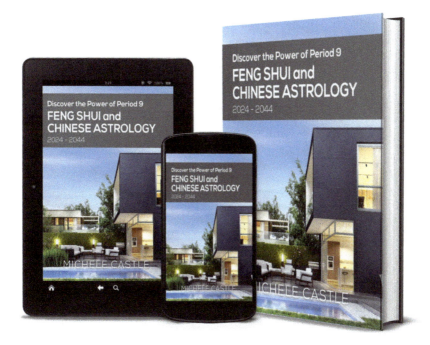

michele@completefengshui.com or visit www.completefengshui.com.

Available Audible, Ebook or hardcover https://amzn.to/47AyeRh

Printed in the USA
CPSIA information can be obtained
at www.ICGtesting.com
LVHW052143100124
768719LV00059B/2169